THE BIG

Order

Book

FOR

SMALL BUSINESS

ORDER FORMS - PLANNER - ORGANIZER

NAME   : _____

BUSINESS : _____

PHONE   : _____

EMAIL   : _____

BOOK NO : _____   DATE : _____

MODERN BIZ PRESS

Content of the Book

Order Reference

This section with order index helps to quickly navigate through order forms, it provides a table to record order number, order summary with page numbers and check box to mark once the order completed.

Monthly Planner & Organizer

This book comes with a 12 month, two page per month monthly planner to comprehensively plan and organize the business. You can use it to track monthly orders, set goals, record expenses, as a to-do list or record special notes of the month. Undated and customizable layout is highly versatile allowing it to be used according to the business needs.

Order summary page can be used for review annual & monthly sales perfermence.

Calendar of the year 2021 & 2022 also has been added for your convenience.

Order Forms

This book contains two types of order forms - one with full page form for large orders and other with half page forms for small orders allowing maximum utilization of the space. Both forms provide a layout to capture orders in full details. Space to record order number, order title, order placing day with full customer information including name, company, address, phone & email. Order detail section can capture, item name, description, quantity, unit price and total. Payment section has space to record sub-total, shipping/delivery charge, total discount, tax and total order value with payment method and payment day. Delivery section has option record tracking number, delivery method with current status of the order. Dedicated note section also being included in the form to capture additional order related information.

Full page order form - 10 items per form   **Half page order forms - 5 items per form**

Calendar 2023

January
Su	Mo	Tu	We	Th	Fr	Sa
1	2	3	4	5	6	7
8	9	10	11	12	13	14
15	16	17	18	19	20	21
22	23	24	25	26	27	28
29	30	31				

6:○ 14:◑ 21:● 28:◐

February
Su	Mo	Tu	We	Th	Fr	Sa
			1	2	3	4
5	6	7	8	9	10	11
12	13	14	15	16	17	18
19	20	21	22	23	24	25
26	27	28				

5:○ 13:◑ 20:● 27:◐

March
Su	Mo	Tu	We	Th	Fr	Sa
			1	2	3	4
5	6	7	8	9	10	11
12	13	14	15	16	17	18
19	20	21	22	23	24	25
26	27	28	29	30	31	

7:○ 14:◑ 21:● 28:◐

April
Su	Mo	Tu	We	Th	Fr	Sa
						1
2	3	4	5	6	7	8
9	10	11	12	13	14	15
16	17	18	19	20	21	22
23	24	25	26	27	28	29
30						

6:○ 13:◑ 20:● 27:◐

May
Su	Mo	Tu	We	Th	Fr	Sa
	1	2	3	4	5	6
7	8	9	10	11	12	13
14	15	16	17	18	19	20
21	22	23	24	25	26	27
28	29	30	31			

5:○ 12:◑ 19:● 27:◐

June
Su	Mo	Tu	We	Th	Fr	Sa
				1	2	3
4	5	6	7	8	9	10
11	12	13	14	15	16	17
18	19	20	21	22	23	24
25	26	27	28	29	30	

3:○ 10:◑ 18:● 26:◐

July
Su	Mo	Tu	We	Th	Fr	Sa
						1
2	3	4	5	6	7	8
9	10	11	12	13	14	15
16	17	18	19	20	21	22
23	24	25	26	27	28	29
30	31					

3:○ 9:◑ 17:● 25:◐

August
Su	Mo	Tu	We	Th	Fr	Sa
		1	2	3	4	5
6	7	8	9	10	11	12
13	14	15	16	17	18	19
20	21	22	23	24	25	26
27	28	29	30	31		

1:○ 8:◑ 16:● 24:◐ 30:○

September
Su	Mo	Tu	We	Th	Fr	Sa
					1	2
3	4	5	6	7	8	9
10	11	12	13	14	15	16
17	18	19	20	21	22	23
24	25	26	27	28	29	30

6:◐ 14:● 22:◑ 29:○

October
Su	Mo	Tu	We	Th	Fr	Sa
1	2	3	4	5	6	7
8	9	10	11	12	13	14
15	16	17	18	19	20	21
22	23	24	25	26	27	28
29	30	31				

6:◐ 14:● 21:◑ 28:○

November
Su	Mo	Tu	We	Th	Fr	Sa
			1	2	3	4
5	6	7	8	9	10	11
12	13	14	15	16	17	18
19	20	21	22	23	24	25
26	27	28	29	30		

5:◐ 13:● 20:◑ 27:○

December
Su	Mo	Tu	We	Th	Fr	Sa
					1	2
3	4	5	6	7	8	9
10	11	12	13	14	15	16
17	18	19	20	21	22	23
24	25	26	27	28	29	30
31						

5:◐ 12:● 19:◑ 26:○

Calendar 2024

January
Su	Mo	Tu	We	Th	Fr	Sa
	1	2	3	4	5	6
7	8	9	10	11	12	13
14	15	16	17	18	19	20
21	22	23	24	25	26	27
28	29	30	31			

3:◐ 11:● 17:◑ 25:○

February
Su	Mo	Tu	We	Th	Fr	Sa
				1	2	3
4	5	6	7	8	9	10
11	12	13	14	15	16	17
18	19	20	21	22	23	24
25	26	27	28	29		

2:◐ 9:● 16:◑ 24:○

March
Su	Mo	Tu	We	Th	Fr	Sa
					1	2
3	4	5	6	7	8	9
10	11	12	13	14	15	16
17	18	19	20	21	22	23
24	25	26	27	28	29	30
31						

3:◐ 10:● 17:◑ 25:○

April
Su	Mo	Tu	We	Th	Fr	Sa
	1	2	3	4	5	6
7	8	9	10	11	12	13
14	15	16	17	18	19	20
21	22	23	24	25	26	27
28	29	30				

1:◐ 8:● 15:◑ 23:○

May
Su	Mo	Tu	We	Th	Fr	Sa
			1	2	3	4
5	6	7	8	9	10	11
12	13	14	15	16	17	18
19	20	21	22	23	24	25
26	27	28	29	30	31	

1:◐ 7:● 15:◑ 23:○ 30:◐

June
Su	Mo	Tu	We	Th	Fr	Sa
						1
2	3	4	5	6	7	8
9	10	11	12	13	14	15
16	17	18	19	20	21	22
23	24	25	26	27	28	29
30						

6:● 14:◑ 21:○ 28:◐

July
Su	Mo	Tu	We	Th	Fr	Sa
	1	2	3	4	5	6
7	8	9	10	11	12	13
14	15	16	17	18	19	20
21	22	23	24	25	26	27
28	29	30	31			

5:● 13:◑ 21:○ 27:◐

August
Su	Mo	Tu	We	Th	Fr	Sa
				1	2	3
4	5	6	7	8	9	10
11	12	13	14	15	16	17
18	19	20	21	22	23	24
25	26	27	28	29	30	31

4:● 12:◑ 19:○ 26:◐

September
Su	Mo	Tu	We	Th	Fr	Sa
1	2	3	4	5	6	7
8	9	10	11	12	13	14
15	16	17	18	19	20	21
22	23	24	25	26	27	28
29	30					

2:● 11:◑ 17:○ 24:◐

October
Su	Mo	Tu	We	Th	Fr	Sa
		1	2	3	4	5
6	7	8	9	10	11	12
13	14	15	16	17	18	19
20	21	22	23	24	25	26
27	28	29	30	31		

2:● 10:◑ 17:○ 24:◐

November
Su	Mo	Tu	We	Th	Fr	Sa
					1	2
3	4	5	6	7	8	9
10	11	12	13	14	15	16
17	18	19	20	21	22	23
24	25	26	27	28	29	30

1:● 9:◑ 15:○ 22:◐

December
Su	Mo	Tu	We	Th	Fr	Sa
1	2	3	4	5	6	7
8	9	10	11	12	13	14
15	16	17	18	19	20	21
22	23	24	25	26	27	28
29	30	31				

1:● 8:◑ 15:○ 22:◐ 30:●

Order Reference

✓	ORDER #	ORDER	PAGE	✓	ORDER #	ORDER	PAGE
☐				☐			
☐				☐			
☐				☐			
☐				☐			
☐				☐			
☐				☐			
☐				☐			
☐				☐			
☐				☐			
☐				☐			
☐				☐			
☐				☐			
☐				☐			
☐				☐			
☐				☐			
☐				☐			
☐				☐			
☐				☐			
☐				☐			
☐				☐			
☐				☐			
☐				☐			
☐				☐			
☐				☐			
☐				☐			
☐				☐			
☐				☐			
☐				☐			
☐				☐			
☐				☐			
☐				☐			
☐				☐			

Order Reference

✓	ORDER #	ORDER	PAGE	✓	ORDER #	ORDER	PAGE
☐				☐			
☐				☐			
☐				☐			
☐				☐			
☐				☐			
☐				☐			
☐				☐			
☐				☐			
☐				☐			
☐				☐			
☐				☐			
☐				☐			
☐				☐			
☐				☐			
☐				☐			
☐				☐			
☐				☐			
☐				☐			
☐				☐			
☐				☐			
☐				☐			
☐				☐			
☐				☐			
☐				☐			
☐				☐			
☐				☐			
☐				☐			
☐				☐			
☐				☐			
☐				☐			
☐				☐			
☐				☐			
☐				☐			

Order Reference

✓	ORDER #	ORDER	PAGE	✓	ORDER #	ORDER	PAGE
☐				☐			
☐				☐			
☐				☐			
☐				☐			
☐				☐			
☐				☐			
☐				☐			
☐				☐			
☐				☐			
☐				☐			
☐				☐			
☐				☐			
☐				☐			
☐				☐			
☐				☐			
☐				☐			
☐				☐			
☐				☐			
☐				☐			
☐				☐			
☐				☐			
☐				☐			
☐				☐			
☐				☐			
☐				☐			
☐				☐			
☐				☐			
☐				☐			
☐				☐			
☐				☐			
☐				☐			
☐				☐			

Monthly Planner

Month/Year : .... **/ 20** ....

SUN	MON	TUE	WED	THU

▶

Notes for the Month

FRI	SAT

- [ ]
- [ ]
- [ ]
- [ ]
- [ ]
- [ ]
- [ ]
- [ ]
- [ ]
- [ ]
- [ ]
- [ ]

- [ ]
- [ ]
- [ ]
- [ ]
- [ ]
- [ ]
- [ ]
- [ ]
- [ ]
- [ ]
- [ ]
- [ ]
- [ ]

▶

Monthly Planner

Month/Year : .... **/ 20** ....

SUN	MON	TUE	WED	THU

▶

....

....

FRI	SAT

Notes for the Month

- [ ]
- [ ]
- [ ]
- [ ]
- [ ]
- [ ]
- [ ]
- [ ]
- [ ]
- [ ]
- [ ]
- [ ]
- [ ]

- [ ]
- [ ]
- [ ]
- [ ]
- [ ]
- [ ]
- [ ]
- [ ]
- [ ]
- [ ]
- [ ]
- [ ]
- [ ]

▶

Monthly Planner

Month/Year : .... **/ 20**

SUN	MON	TUE	WED	THU

▶

Notes for the Month

FRI	SAT

- ☐
- ☐
- ☐
- ☐
- ☐
- ☐
- ☐
- ☐
- ☐
- ☐
- ☐
- ☐
- ☐

- ☐
- ☐
- ☐
- ☐
- ☐
- ☐
- ☐
- ☐
- ☐
- ☐
- ☐
- ☐
- ☐

▶

Monthly Planner

Month/Year : .... **/ 20** ....

SUN	MON	TUE	WED	THU

▶

....

....

FRI	SAT

Notes for the Month

- [ ]
- [ ]
- [ ]
- [ ]
- [ ]
- [ ]
- [ ]
- [ ]
- [ ]
- [ ]
- [ ]
- [ ]
- [ ]

- [ ]
- [ ]
- [ ]
- [ ]
- [ ]
- [ ]
- [ ]
- [ ]
- [ ]
- [ ]
- [ ]
- [ ]
- [ ]
- [ ]
- [ ]

▶

Monthly Planner

Month/Year : .... **/ 20** ....

SUN	MON	TUE	WED	THU

▶

....
....
....

Notes for the Month

FRI	SAT

- [ ]
- [ ]
- [ ]
- [ ]
- [ ]
- [ ]
- [ ]
- [ ]
- [ ]
- [ ]
- [ ]
- [ ]
- [ ]

- [ ]
- [ ]
- [ ]
- [ ]
- [ ]
- [ ]
- [ ]
- [ ]
- [ ]
- [ ]
- [ ]
- [ ]
- [ ]
- [ ]

▶

Monthly Planner

Month/Year : .... **/ 20** ....

SUN	MON	TUE	WED	THU

▶

....

....

FRI	SAT

▶

Monthly Planner

Month/Year : .... **/ 20** ....

SUN	MON	TUE	WED	THU

▶

Notes for the Month

FRI	SAT

- [ ]
- [ ]
- [ ]
- [ ]
- [ ]
- [ ]
- [ ]
- [ ]
- [ ]
- [ ]
- [ ]
- [ ]
- [ ]

- [ ]
- [ ]
- [ ]
- [ ]
- [ ]
- [ ]
- [ ]
- [ ]
- [ ]
- [ ]
- [ ]
- [ ]
- [ ]

▶

Monthly Planner

Month/Year : .... **/ 20** ....

SUN	MON	TUE	WED	THU

▶

....

....

....

Notes for the Month

FRI	SAT

▶

Monthly Planner

Month/Year : .... **/ 20** ....

SUN	MON	TUE	WED	THU

▶

Notes for the Month

FRI	SAT

- [ ]
- [ ]
- [ ]
- [ ]
- [ ]
- [ ]
- [ ]
- [ ]
- [ ]
- [ ]
- [ ]
- [ ]
- [ ]

- [ ]
- [ ]
- [ ]
- [ ]
- [ ]
- [ ]
- [ ]
- [ ]
- [ ]
- [ ]
- [ ]
- [ ]
- [ ]

▶

Monthly Planner

Month/Year : .... **/ 20** ....

SUN	MON	TUE	WED	THU

▶

....

....

....

Notes for the Month

FRI	SAT

☐
☐
☐
☐
☐
☐
☐
☐
☐
☐
☐
☐
☐

☐
☐
☐
☐
☐
☐
☐
☐
☐
☐
☐
☐
☐
☐

▶

Monthly Planner

Month/Year : .... **/ 20** ....

SUN	MON	TUE	WED	THU

►

Notes for the Month

FRI	SAT

- [ ]
- [ ]
- [ ]
- [ ]
- [ ]
- [ ]
- [ ]
- [ ]
- [ ]
- [ ]
- [ ]
- [ ]
- [ ]

- [ ]
- [ ]
- [ ]
- [ ]
- [ ]
- [ ]
- [ ]
- [ ]
- [ ]
- [ ]
- [ ]
- [ ]
- [ ]
- [ ]

▶

Monthly Planner

Month/Year : .... **/ 20** ....

SUN	MON	TUE	WED	THU

▶

....

....

....

Notes for the Month

FRI	SAT

▶

Order Summary

MONTH	NO. OF ORDERS	ORDER VALUE	SHIPPING	DISCOUNTS	TOTAL
TOTAL					

Order Form

ORDER NO:

DATE:

ORDER NAME:

✓

Customer Details

Name :

Company:

Phone: Email :

Address:

Order Details

#	Item/Description	Qty	Price	Discount	Total
☐					
☐					
☐					
☐					
☐					
☐					
☐					
☐					
☐					
☐					

TOTAL

Payment Details

Subtotal :

Delivery :

Discount:

TAX   :

Date

Total

Status
☐ Paid   ☐ Half Paid   ☐ Pending

Payment Method
☐ Cash   ☐ Credit Card   ☐ Bank   ☐ PayPal
☐ Other :

Delivery Details

Delivery Date :

Method   :   ☐ Pick-up   ☐ Delivery

Tracking No

Status
☐ Started   ☐ Finished   ☐ Delivered

Special Notes

Order Form

ORDER NO:

DATE:

ORDER NAME:

✓

Customer Details

Name :

Company:

Phone:

Email :

Address:

Order Details

	#	Item/Description	Qty	Price	Discount	Total
☐						
☐						
☐						
☐						
☐						
☐						
☐						
☐						
☐						
☐						
☐						

TOTAL

Payment Details

Subtotal :

Delivery :

Discount:

TAX   :

Date

Total

Status
☐ Paid   ☐ Half Paid   ☐ Pending

Payment Method
☐ Cash   ☐ Credit Card   ☐ Bank   ☐ PayPal
☐ Other :

Special Notes

Delivery Details

Delivery Date :

Method   :   ☐ Pick-up   ☐ Delivery

Tracking No

Status
☐ Started   ☐ Finished   ☐ Delivered

Order Form

ORDER NO:

DATE:

ORDER NAME:

✓

Customer Details

Name :

Company:

Phone: Email :

Address:

Order Details

#	Item/Description	Qty	Price	Discount	Total
☐					
☐					
☐					
☐					
☐					
☐					
☐					
☐					
☐					
☐					

TOTAL

Payment Details

Subtotal :

Delivery :

Discount:

TAX   :

Date

Total

Status
☐ Paid   ☐ Half Paid   ☐ Pending

Payment Method
☐ Cash   ☐ Credit Card   ☐ Bank   ☐ PayPal
☐ Other :

Delivery Details

Delivery Date :

Method   :   ☐ Pick-up   ☐ Delivery

Tracking No

Status
☐ Started   ☐ Finished   ☐ Delivered

Special Notes

Order Form - Small Orders

Name : _____

Address: _____

Phone: _____ **Email :** _____

ORDER NO: _____

DATE: _____

ORDER NAME: _____ ✓

Order Details

#	Item/Description	Qty	Price	Discount	Total
☐					
☐					
☐					
☐					
☐					

Notes:

TOTAL

Payment Details

Subtotal : _____

Delivery : _____

Discount: _____ **TAX:** _____

Method : _____

Date

Total

Status
☐ Paid ☐ Half Paid ☐ Pending

Delivery Details

Delivery Date : _____

Method : ☐ Pick-up ☐ Delivery

Tracking No

Status
☐ Started ☐ Finished ☐ Delivered

Order Form - Small Orders

Name : _____

Address: _____

Phone: _____ **Email :** _____

ORDER NO: _____

DATE: _____

ORDER NAME: _____ ✓

Order Details

#	Item/Description	Qty	Price	Discount	Total
☐					
☐					
☐					
☐					
☐					

Notes:

TOTAL

Payment Details

Subtotal : _____

Delivery : _____

Discount: _____ **TAX:** _____

Method : _____

Date

Total

Status
☐ Paid ☐ Half Paid ☐ Pending

Delivery Details

Delivery Date : _____

Method : ☐ Pick-up ☐ Delivery

Tracking No

Status
☐ Started ☐ Finished ☐ Delivered

Order Form

ORDER NO:

DATE:

ORDER NAME:

✓

Customer Details

Name :

Company:

Phone: Email :

Address:

Order Details

	#	Item/Description	Qty	Price	Discount	Total
☐						
☐						
☐						
☐						
☐						
☐						
☐						
☐						
☐						
☐						

TOTAL

Payment Details

Subtotal :

Delivery :

Discount :

TAX   :

Date

Total

Status
☐ Paid   ☐ Half Paid   ☐ Pending

Payment Method
☐ Cash ☐ Credit Card ☐ Bank ☐ PayPal
☐ Other :

Special Notes

Delivery Details

Delivery Date :

Method   : ☐ Pick-up   ☐ Delivery

Tracking No

Status
☐ Started   ☐ Finished   ☐ Delivered

Order Form

ORDER NO:

DATE:

ORDER NAME:

✓

Customer Details

Name :

Address:

Company:

Phone: Email :

Order Details

#	Item/Description	Qty	Price	Discount	Total
☐					
☐					
☐					
☐					
☐					
☐					
☐					
☐					
☐					
☐					

TOTAL

Payment Details

Subtotal :

Delivery :

Discount :

TAX   :

Date

Total

Status

☐ Paid   ☐ Half Paid   ☐ Pending

Payment Method

☐ Cash   ☐ Credit Card   ☐ Bank   ☐ PayPal

☐ Other :

Delivery Details

Delivery Date :

Method   :   ☐ Pick-up   ☐ Delivery

Tracking No

Status

☐ Started   ☐ Finished   ☐ Delivered

Special Notes

Order Form

ORDER NO:

DATE:

ORDER NAME:

✓

Customer Details

Name :

Address:

Company:

Phone:

Email :

Order Details

	#	Item/Description	Qty	Price	Discount	Total
☐						
☐						
☐						
☐						
☐						
☐						
☐						
☐						
☐						
☐						

TOTAL

Payment Details

Subtotal :

Delivery :

Discount :

TAX　　　 :

Date

Total

Status
☐ Paid　☐ Half Paid　☐ Pending

Payment Method
☐ Cash　☐ Credit Card　☐ Bank　☐ PayPal
☐ Other :

Special Notes

Delivery Details

Delivery Date :

Method　　　 :　☐ Pick-up　☐ Delivery

Tracking No

Status
☐ Started　☐ Finished　☐ Delivered

Order Form - Small Orders

Name :

Address:

Phone: **Email :**

ORDER NO:

DATE:

ORDER NAME: ✓

Order Details

#	Item/Description	Qty	Price	Discount	Total
☐					
☐					
☐					
☐					
☐					

Notes: **TOTAL**

Payment Details

Subtotal :

Delivery :

Discount : **TAX:**

Method :

Date

Total

Status
☐ Paid ☐ Half Paid ☐ Pending

Delivery Details

Delivery Date :

Method : ☐ Pick-up ☐ Delivery

Tracking No

Status
☐ Started ☐ Finished ☐ Delivered

Order Form - Small Orders

Name :

Address:

Phone: **Email :**

ORDER NO:

DATE:

ORDER NAME: ✓

Order Details

#	Item/Description	Qty	Price	Discount	Total
☐					
☐					
☐					
☐					
☐					

Notes: **TOTAL**

Payment Details

Subtotal :

Delivery :

Discount : **TAX:**

Method :

Date

Total

Status
☐ Paid ☐ Half Paid ☐ Pending

Delivery Details

Delivery Date :

Method : ☐ Pick-up ☐ Delivery

Tracking No

Status
☐ Started ☐ Finished ☐ Delivered

Order Form

ORDER NO:

DATE:

ORDER NAME:

✓

Customer Details

Name :

Company:

Phone: Email :

Address:

Order Details

	#	Item/Description	Qty	Price	Discount	Total
☐						
☐						
☐						
☐						
☐						
☐						
☐						
☐						
☐						
☐						

TOTAL

Payment Details

Subtotal :

Delivery :

Discount :

TAX   :

Date

Total

Status
☐ Paid   ☐ Half Paid   ☐ Pending

Payment Method
☐ Cash   ☐ Credit Card   ☐ Bank   ☐ PayPal
☐ Other :

Delivery Details

Delivery Date :

Method   : ☐ Pick-up   ☐ Delivery

Tracking No

Status
☐ Started   ☐ Finished   ☐ Delivered

Special Notes

Order Form

ORDER NO:

DATE:

ORDER NAME:

✓

Customer Details

Name :

Company:

Phone:

Email :

Address:

Order Details

#	Item/Description	Qty	Price	Discount	Total
☐					
☐					
☐					
☐					
☐					
☐					
☐					
☐					
☐					
☐					

TOTAL

Payment Details

Subtotal :

Delivery :

Discount :

TAX :

Date

Total

Status

☐ Paid   ☐ Half Paid   ☐ Pending

┌ Payment Method ─────────────────┐
☐ Cash   ☐ Credit Card   ☐ Bank   ☐ PayPal

☐ Other :

Delivery Details

Delivery Date :

Method : ☐ Pick-up   ☐ Delivery

┌ Tracking No ─┐ ┌── Status ──┐
                  ☐ Started   ☐ Finished   ☐ Delivered

Special Notes

Order Form

ORDER NO:

DATE:

ORDER NAME:

✓

Customer Details

Name :

Company:

Phone:

Email :

Address:

Order Details

	#	Item/Description	Qty	Price	Discount	Total
☐						
☐						
☐						
☐						
☐						
☐						
☐						
☐						
☐						
☐						

TOTAL

Payment Details

Subtotal :

Delivery :

Discount :

TAX :

Date

Total

Status

☐ Paid ☐ Half Paid ☐ Pending

Payment Method

☐ Cash ☐ Credit Card ☐ Bank ☐ PayPal

☐ Other :

Special Notes

Delivery Details

Delivery Date :

Method : ☐ Pick-up ☐ Delivery

Tracking No

Status

☐ Started ☐ Finished ☐ Delivered

Order Form - Small Orders

Name :

Address:

Phone: **Email :**

ORDER NO:

DATE:

ORDER NAME: ✓

Order Details

#	Item/Description	Qty	Price	Discount	Total
☐					
☐					
☐					
☐					
☐					

Notes: **TOTAL**

Payment Details

Subtotal :

Delivery :

Discount :   **TAX:**

Method :

Date

Total

Status
☐ Paid   ☐ Half Paid   ☐ Pending

Delivery Details

Delivery Date :

Method : ☐ Pick-up   ☐ Delivery

Tracking No

Status
☐ Started   ☐ Finished   ☐ Delivered

Order Form - Small Orders

Name :

Address:

Phone: **Email :**

ORDER NO:

DATE:

ORDER NAME: ✓

Order Details

#	Item/Description	Qty	Price	Discount	Total
☐					
☐					
☐					
☐					
☐					

Notes: **TOTAL**

Payment Details

Subtotal :

Delivery :

Discount :   **TAX:**

Method :

Date

Total

Status
☐ Paid   ☐ Half Paid   ☐ Pending

Delivery Details

Delivery Date :

Method : ☐ Pick-up   ☐ Delivery

Tracking No

Status
☐ Started   ☐ Finished   ☐ Delivered

Order Form

ORDER NO:

DATE:

ORDER NAME:

✓

Customer Details

Name :

Company:

Phone: Email :

Address:

Order Details

	#	Item/Description	Qty	Price	Discount	Total
☐						
☐						
☐						
☐						
☐						
☐						
☐						
☐						
☐						
☐						

TOTAL

Payment Details

Subtotal :

Delivery :

Discount :

TAX   :

Date

Total

Status

☐ Paid   ☐ Half Paid   ☐ Pending

Payment Method

☐ Cash   ☐ Credit Card   ☐ Bank   ☐ PayPal

☐ Other :

Special Notes

Delivery Details

Delivery Date :

Method   :   ☐ Pick-up   ☐ Delivery

Tracking No

Status

☐ Started   ☐ Finished   ☐ Delivered

Order Form

ORDER NO: _____

DATE: _____

ORDER NAME: _____ ✓ ☐

Customer Details

Name : _____

Company: _____

Phone: _____ Email : _____

Address:
_____
_____
_____

Order Details

#	Item/Description	Qty	Price	Discount	Total
☐					
☐					
☐					
☐					
☐					
☐					
☐					
☐					
☐					
☐					

TOTAL _____

Payment Details

Subtotal : _____

Delivery : _____

Discount : _____

TAX : _____

Date _____

Total _____

Status
☐ Paid   ☐ Half Paid   ☐ Pending

Payment Method

☐ Cash ☐ Credit Card ☐ Bank ☐ PayPal

☐ Other : _____

Delivery Details

Delivery Date : _____

Method : ☐ Pick-up ☐ Delivery

Tracking No
_____

Status
☐ Started ☐ Finished ☐ Delivered

Special Notes

Order Form

ORDER NO:

DATE:

ORDER NAME:

✓

Customer Details

Name :

Address:

Company:

Phone: Email :

Order Details

☐	#	Item/Description	Qty	Price	Discount	Total
☐						
☐						
☐						
☐						
☐						
☐						
☐						
☐						
☐						
☐						

TOTAL

Payment Details

Date

Subtotal :

Delivery :

Total

Discount:

TAX   :

Status

☐ Paid   ☐ Half Paid   ☐ Pending

Payment Method

☐ Cash   ☐ Credit Card   ☐ Bank   ☐ PayPal

☐ Other :

Special Notes

Delivery Details

Delivery Date :

Method   :   ☐ Pick-up   ☐ Delivery

Tracking No

Status

☐ Started   ☐ Finished   ☐ Delivered

Order Form - Small Orders

Name :

Address:

Phone: **Email :**

ORDER NO:

DATE:

ORDER NAME: ✓

Order Details

	#	Item/Description	Qty	Price	Discount	Total
☐						
☐						
☐						
☐						
☐						

Notes: **TOTAL**

Payment Details

Subtotal :

Delivery :

Discount: **TAX:**

Method :

Date

Total

Status
☐ Paid   ☐ Half Paid   ☐ Pending

Delivery Details

Delivery Date :

Method :   ☐ Pick-up   ☐ Delivery

Tracking No

Status
☐ Started   ☐ Finished   ☐ Delivered

Order Form - Small Orders

Name :

Address:

Phone: **Email :**

ORDER NO:

DATE:

ORDER NAME: ✓

Order Details

	#	Item/Description	Qty	Price	Discount	Total
☐						
☐						
☐						
☐						
☐						

Notes: **TOTAL**

Payment Details

Subtotal :

Delivery :

Discount: **TAX:**

Method :

Date

Total

Status
☐ Paid   ☐ Half Paid   ☐ Pending

Delivery Details

Delivery Date :

Method :   ☐ Pick-up   ☐ Delivery

Tracking No

Status
☐ Started   ☐ Finished   ☐ Delivered

Order Form

ORDER NO:

DATE:

ORDER NAME:

✓

Customer Details

Name :

Company:

Phone: Email :

Address:

Order Details

	#	Item/Description	Qty	Price	Discount	Total
☐						
☐						
☐						
☐						
☐						
☐						
☐						
☐						
☐						
☐						
					TOTAL	

Payment Details

Subtotal :

Delivery :

Discount :

TAX   :

Date

Total

Status

☐ Paid   ☐ Half Paid   ☐ Pending

Payment Method
☐ Cash ☐ Credit Card ☐ Bank ☐ PayPal
☐ Other :

Delivery Details

Delivery Date :

Method   :   ☐ Pick-up   ☐ Delivery

Tracking No   Status
☐ Started   ☐ Finished   ☐ Delivered

Special Notes

Order Form

ORDER NO:

DATE:

ORDER NAME:

✓

Customer Details

Name :

Company:

Phone: Email :

Address:

Order Details

	#	Item/Description	Qty	Price	Discount	Total
☐						
☐						
☐						
☐						
☐						
☐						
☐						
☐						
☐						
☐						
					TOTAL	

Payment Details

Subtotal :

Delivery :

Discount :

TAX   :

Date

Total

Status

☐ Paid ☐ Half Paid ☐ Pending

Payment Method

☐ Cash ☐ Credit Card ☐ Bank ☐ PayPal

☐ Other :

Delivery Details

Delivery Date :

Method   : ☐ Pick-up ☐ Delivery

Tracking No

Status

☐ Started ☐ Finished ☐ Delivered

Special Notes

Order Form

ORDER NO:

DATE:

ORDER NAME:

✓

Customer Details

Name :

Company:

Phone: Email :

Address:

Order Details

☐	#	Item/Description	Qty	Price	Discount	Total
☐						
☐						
☐						
☐						
☐						
☐						
☐						
☐						
☐						
☐						

TOTAL

Payment Details

Subtotal :

Delivery :

Discount :

TAX   :

Date

Total

Status
☐ Paid   ☐ Half Paid   ☐ Pending

Payment Method
☐ Cash ☐ Credit Card ☐ Bank ☐ PayPal
☐ Other :

Delivery Details

Delivery Date :

Method   :   ☐ Pick-up   ☐ Delivery

Tracking No

Status
☐ Started   ☐ Finished   ☐ Delivered

Special Notes

Order Form - Small Orders

Name :

Address:

Phone: **Email :**

ORDER NO:

DATE:

ORDER NAME: ✓

Order Details

#	Item/Description	Qty	Price	Discount	Total
☐					
☐					
☐					
☐					
☐					

Notes: **TOTAL**

Payment Details

Subtotal :

Delivery :

Discount: **TAX:**

Method :

Date

Total

Status
☐ Paid ☐ Half Paid ☐ Pending

Delivery Details

Delivery Date :

Method   : ☐ Pick-up ☐ Delivery

Tracking No

Status
☐ Started ☐ Finished ☐ Delivered

Order Form - Small Orders

Name :

Address:

Phone: **Email :**

ORDER NO:

DATE:

ORDER NAME: ✓

Order Details

#	Item/Description	Qty	Price	Discount	Total
☐					
☐					
☐					
☐					
☐					

Notes: **TOTAL**

Payment Details

Subtotal :

Delivery :

Discount: **TAX:**

Method :

Date

Total

Status
☐ Paid ☐ Half Paid ☐ Pending

Delivery Details

Delivery Date :

Method   : ☐ Pick-up ☐ Delivery

Tracking No

Status
☐ Started ☐ Finished ☐ Delivered

Order Form

ORDER NO:

DATE:

ORDER NAME:

✓

Customer Details

Name :

Company:

Phone:

Email :

Address:

Order Details

	#	Item/Description	Qty	Price	Discount	Total
☐						
☐						
☐						
☐						
☐						
☐						
☐						
☐						
☐						
☐						

TOTAL

Payment Details

Subtotal :

Delivery :

Discount :

TAX :

Date

Total

Status

☐ Paid   ☐ Half Paid   ☐ Pending

Payment Method

☐ Cash   ☐ Credit Card   ☐ Bank   ☐ PayPal

☐ Other :

Special Notes

Delivery Details

Delivery Date :

Method : ☐ Pick-up   ☐ Delivery

Tracking No

Status

☐ Started   ☐ Finished   ☐ Delivered

Order Form

ORDER NO:

DATE:

ORDER NAME:

✓

Customer Details

Name :

Address:

Company:

Phone:

Email :

Order Details

#	Item/Description	Qty	Price	Discount	Total
☐					
☐					
☐					
☐					
☐					
☐					
☐					
☐					
☐					
☐					

TOTAL

Payment Details

Subtotal :

Delivery :

Discount :

TAX   :

Date

Total

Status

☐ Paid   ☐ Half Paid   ☐ Pending

Payment Method

☐ Cash   ☐ Credit Card   ☐ Bank   ☐ PayPal

☐ Other :

Delivery Details

Delivery Date :

Method   :   ☐ Pick-up   ☐ Delivery

Tracking No

Status

☐ Started   ☐ Finished   ☐ Delivered

Special Notes

Order Form

ORDER NO:

DATE:

ORDER NAME:

✓

Customer Details

Name :

Company:

Phone: Email :

Address:

Order Details

	#	Item/Description	Qty	Price	Discount	Total
☐						
☐						
☐						
☐						
☐						
☐						
☐						
☐						
☐						
☐						

TOTAL

Payment Details

Subtotal :

Delivery :

Discount:

TAX   :

Date

Total

Status

☐ Paid   ☐ Half Paid   ☐ Pending

Payment Method

☐ Cash   ☐ Credit Card   ☐ Bank   ☐ PayPal

☐ Other :

Delivery Details

Delivery Date :

Method   :   ☐ Pick-up   ☐ Delivery

Tracking No

Status

☐ Started   ☐ Finished   ☐ Delivered

Special Notes

Order Form - Small Orders

Name :

Address:

Phone: Email :

ORDER NO:

DATE:

ORDER NAME:

✓

Order Details

#	Item/Description	Qty	Price	Discount	Total
☐					
☐					
☐					
☐					
☐					

Notes: **TOTAL**

Payment Details

Subtotal :

Delivery :

Discount: TAX:

Method   :

Date

Total

Status
☐ Paid ☐ Half Paid ☐ Pending

Delivery Details

Delivery Date :

Method   : ☐ Pick-up ☐ Delivery

Tracking No

Status
☐ Started ☐ Finished ☐ Delivered

Order Form - Small Orders

Name :

Address:

Phone: Email :

ORDER NO:

DATE:

ORDER NAME:

✓

Order Details

#	Item/Description	Qty	Price	Discount	Total
☐					
☐					
☐					
☐					
☐					

Notes: **TOTAL**

Payment Details

Subtotal :

Delivery :

Discount: TAX:

Method   :

Date

Total

Status
☐ Paid ☐ Half Paid ☐ Pending

Delivery Details

Delivery Date :

Method   : ☐ Pick-up ☐ Delivery

Tracking No

Status
☐ Started ☐ Finished ☐ Delivered

Order Form

ORDER NO:

DATE:

ORDER NAME:

✓

Customer Details

Name :

Address:

Company:

Phone: Email :

Order Details

	#	Item/Description	Qty	Price	Discount	Total
☐						
☐						
☐						
☐						
☐						
☐						
☐						
☐						
☐						
☐						

TOTAL

Payment Details

Subtotal :

Delivery :

Discount :

TAX   :

Date

Total

Status

☐ Paid   ☐ Half Paid   ☐ Pending

Payment Method

☐ Cash   ☐ Credit Card   ☐ Bank   ☐ PayPal

☐ Other :

Special Notes

Delivery Details

Delivery Date :

Method   :   ☐ Pick-up   ☐ Delivery

Tracking No

Status

☐ Started   ☐ Finished   ☐ Delivered

Order Form

ORDER NO:

DATE:

ORDER NAME:

✓

Customer Details

Name :

Company:

Phone: Email :

Address:

Order Details

	#	Item/Description	Qty	Price	Discount	Total
☐						
☐						
☐						
☐						
☐						
☐						
☐						
☐						
☐						
☐						

TOTAL

Payment Details

Subtotal :

Delivery :

Discount :

TAX   :

Date

Total

Status
☐ Paid   ☐ Half Paid   ☐ Pending

Payment Method
☐ Cash   ☐ Credit Card   ☐ Bank   ☐ PayPal
☐ Other :

Delivery Details

Delivery Date :

Method   :   ☐ Pick-up   ☐ Delivery

Tracking No

Status
☐ Started   ☐ Finished   ☐ Delivered

Special Notes

Order Form

ORDER NO:

DATE:

ORDER NAME:

✓

Customer Details

Name :

Company:

Phone:

Email :

Address:

Order Details

#	Item/Description	Qty	Price	Discount	Total
☐					
☐					
☐					
☐					
☐					
☐					
☐					
☐					
☐					
☐					

TOTAL

Payment Details

Subtotal :

Delivery :

Discount:

TAX :

Date

Total

Status

☐ Paid ☐ Half Paid ☐ Pending

Payment Method

☐ Cash ☐ Credit Card ☐ Bank ☐ PayPal

☐ Other :

Delivery Details

Delivery Date :

Method : ☐ Pick-up ☐ Delivery

Tracking No

Status

☐ Started ☐ Finished ☐ Delivered

Special Notes

Order Form - Small Orders

Name :

Address:

Phone: **Email :**

ORDER NO:

DATE:

ORDER NAME: ✓

Order Details

#	Item/Description	Qty	Price	Discount	Total
☐					
☐					
☐					
☐					
☐					

Notes: **TOTAL**

Payment Details

Subtotal :

Delivery :

Discount: **TAX:**

Method :

Date

Total

Status
☐ Paid   ☐ Half Paid   ☐ Pending

Delivery Details

Delivery Date :

Method : ☐ Pick-up ☐ Delivery

Tracking No

Status
☐ Started   ☐ Finished   ☐ Delivered

Order Form - Small Orders

Name :

Address:

Phone: **Email :**

ORDER NO:

DATE:

ORDER NAME: ✓

Order Details

#	Item/Description	Qty	Price	Discount	Total
☐					
☐					
☐					
☐					
☐					

Notes: **TOTAL**

Payment Details

Subtotal :

Delivery :

Discount: **TAX:**

Method :

Date

Total

Status
☐ Paid   ☐ Half Paid   ☐ Pending

Delivery Details

Delivery Date :

Method : ☐ Pick-up ☐ Delivery

Tracking No

Status
☐ Started   ☐ Finished   ☐ Delivered

Order Form

ORDER NO:

DATE:

ORDER NAME:

✓

Customer Details

Name :

Company:

Phone:

Email :

Address:

Order Details

	#	Item/Description	Qty	Price	Discount	Total
☐						
☐						
☐						
☐						
☐						
☐						
☐						
☐						
☐						
☐						

TOTAL

Payment Details

Subtotal :

Delivery :

Discount :

TAX :

Date

Total

Status

☐ Paid   ☐ Half Paid   ☐ Pending

┌ Payment Method ─────────────────┐
☐ Cash   ☐ Credit Card   ☐ Bank   ☐ PayPal
☐ Other :

Special Notes

Delivery Details

Delivery Date :

Method : ☐ Pick-up ☐ Delivery

┌ Tracking No ──┐ ┌ Status ──────────┐
                  ☐   ☐   ☐
                  Started   Finished   Delivered

Order Form

ORDER NO:

DATE:

ORDER NAME:

✓

Customer Details

Name :

Address:

Company:

Phone:

Email :

Order Details

#	Item/Description	Qty	Price	Discount	Total
☐					
☐					
☐					
☐					
☐					
☐					
☐					
☐					
☐					
☐					

TOTAL

Payment Details

Subtotal :

Delivery :

Discount:

TAX :

Date

Total

Status

☐ Paid ☐ Half Paid ☐ Pending

Payment Method

☐ Cash ☐ Credit Card ☐ Bank ☐ PayPal

☐ Other :

Delivery Details

Delivery Date :

Method : ☐ Pick-up ☐ Delivery

Tracking No

Status

☐ Started ☐ Finished ☐ Delivered

Special Notes

Order Form

ORDER NO:

DATE:

ORDER NAME:

✓

Customer Details

Name :

Address:

Company:

Phone:

Email :

Order Details

#	Item/Description	Qty	Price	Discount	Total
☐					
☐					
☐					
☐					
☐					
☐					
☐					
☐					
☐					
☐					
				TOTAL	

Payment Details

Date

Subtotal :

Total

Delivery :

Discount :

Status

TAX   :

☐ Paid   ☐ Half Paid   ☐ Pending

Payment Method

☐ Cash ☐ Credit Card ☐ Bank ☐ PayPal

☐ Other :

Special Notes

Delivery Details

Delivery Date :

Method   : ☐ Pick-up   ☐ Delivery

Tracking No

Status

☐ Started   ☐ Finished   ☐ Delivered

Order Form - Small Orders

Name :

Address:

Phone:　　　　　　　　Email :

ORDER NO:

DATE:

ORDER NAME:　　　　　　　　　　　　　✓

Order Details

#	Item/Description	Qty	Price	Discount	Total
☐					
☐					
☐					
☐					
☐					

Notes:　　　　　　　　　　　　　　　**TOTAL**

Payment Details

Subtotal :

Delivery :

Discount:　　　TAX:

Method　:

Date

Total

Status
☐ Paid　☐ Half Paid　☐ Pending

Delivery Details

Delivery Date :

Method　　　:　☐ Pick-up　☐ Delivery

Tracking No

Status
☐ Started　☐ Finished　☐ Delivered

Order Form - Small Orders

Name :

Address:

Phone:　　　　　　　　Email :

ORDER NO:

DATE:

ORDER NAME:　　　　　　　　　　　　　✓

Order Details

#	Item/Description	Qty	Price	Discount	Total
☐					
☐					
☐					
☐					
☐					

Notes:　　　　　　　　　　　　　　　**TOTAL**

Payment Details

Subtotal :

Delivery :

Discount:　　　TAX:

Method　:

Date

Total

Status
☐ Paid　☐ Half Paid　☐ Pending

Delivery Details

Delivery Date :

Method　　　:　☐ Pick-up　☐ Delivery

Tracking No

Status
☐ Started　☐ Finished　☐ Delivered

Order Form

ORDER NO:

DATE:

ORDER NAME:

✓

Customer Details

Name :

Company:

Phone: Email :

Address:

Order Details

	#	Item/Description	Qty	Price	Discount	Total
☐						
☐						
☐						
☐						
☐						
☐						
☐						
☐						
☐						
☐						

TOTAL

Payment Details

Subtotal :

Delivery :

Discount :

TAX   :

Date

Total

Status
☐ Paid   ☐ Half Paid   ☐ Pending

Payment Method
☐ Cash   ☐ Credit Card   ☐ Bank   ☐ PayPal
☐ Other :

Special Notes

Delivery Details

Delivery Date :

Method   :   ☐ Pick-up   ☐ Delivery

Tracking No

Status
☐ Started   ☐ Finished   ☐ Delivered

Order Form

ORDER NO:

DATE:

ORDER NAME:

✓

Customer Details

Name :

Company:

Phone: Email :

Address:

Order Details

#	Item/Description	Qty	Price	Discount	Total
☐					
☐					
☐					
☐					
☐					
☐					
☐					
☐					
☐					
☐					

TOTAL

Payment Details

Subtotal :

Delivery :

Discount:

TAX   :

Date

Total

Status

☐ Paid   ☐ Half Paid   ☐ Pending

Payment Method

☐ Cash   ☐ Credit Card   ☐ Bank   ☐ PayPal

☐ Other :

Delivery Details

Delivery Date :

Method   :   ☐ Pick-up   ☐ Delivery

Tracking No

Status

☐ Started   ☐ Finished   ☐ Delivered

Special Notes

Order Form

ORDER NO:

DATE:

ORDER NAME:

✓

Customer Details

Name :

Address:

Company:

Phone:

Email :

Order Details

	#	Item/Description	Qty	Price	Discount	Total
☐						
☐						
☐						
☐						
☐						
☐						
☐						
☐						
☐						
☐						

TOTAL

Payment Details

Date

Subtotal :

Total

Delivery :

Discount:

TAX   :

Status

☐ Paid   ☐ Half Paid   ☐ Pending

Payment Method

☐ Cash   ☐ Credit Card   ☐ Bank   ☐ PayPal

☐ Other :

Special Notes

Delivery Details

Delivery Date :

Method   :   ☐ Pick-up   ☐ Delivery

Tracking No

Status

☐ Started   ☐ Finished   ☐ Delivered

Order Form - Small Orders

Name :

Address:

Phone: Email :

ORDER NO:

DATE:

ORDER NAME: ✓

Order Details

#	Item/Description	Qty	Price	Discount	Total
☐					
☐					
☐					
☐					
☐					

Notes: **TOTAL**

Payment Details

Subtotal :

Delivery :

Discount: TAX:

Method :

Date

Total

Status
☐ Paid   ☐ Half Paid   ☐ Pending

Delivery Details

Delivery Date :

Method   : ☐ Pick-up   ☐ Delivery

Tracking No

Status
☐ Started   ☐ Finished   ☐ Delivered

Order Form - Small Orders

Name :

Address:

Phone: Email :

ORDER NO:

DATE:

ORDER NAME: ✓

Order Details

#	Item/Description	Qty	Price	Discount	Total
☐					
☐					
☐					
☐					
☐					

Notes: **TOTAL**

Payment Details

Subtotal :

Delivery :

Discount: TAX:

Method :

Date

Total

Status
☐ Paid   ☐ Half Paid   ☐ Pending

Delivery Details

Delivery Date :

Method   : ☐ Pick-up   ☐ Delivery

Tracking No

Status
☐ Started   ☐ Finished   ☐ Delivered

Order Form

ORDER NO:

DATE:

ORDER NAME:

✓

Customer Details

Name :

Company:

Phone:

Email :

Address:

Order Details

	#	Item/Description	Qty	Price	Discount	Total
☐						
☐						
☐						
☐						
☐						
☐						
☐						
☐						
☐						
☐						
					TOTAL	

Payment Details

Subtotal :

Delivery :

Discount :

TAX :

Date

Total

Status

☐ Paid ☐ Half Paid ☐ Pending

Payment Method

☐ Cash ☐ Credit Card ☐ Bank ☐ PayPal

☐ Other :

Special Notes

Delivery Details

Delivery Date :

Method : ☐ Pick-up ☐ Delivery

Tracking No

Status

☐ Started ☐ Finished ☐ Delivered

Order Form

ORDER NO:

DATE:

ORDER NAME:

✓

Customer Details

Name :

Company:

Phone: Email :

Address:

Order Details

#	Item/Description	Qty	Price	Discount	Total
☐					
☐					
☐					
☐					
☐					
☐					
☐					
☐					
☐					
☐					

TOTAL

Payment Details

Subtotal :

Delivery :

Discount :

TAX   :

Date

Total

Status

☐ Paid   ☐ Half Paid   ☐ Pending

Payment Method

☐ Cash   ☐ Credit Card   ☐ Bank   ☐ PayPal

☐ Other :

Special Notes

Delivery Details

Delivery Date :

Method   :   ☐ Pick-up   ☐ Delivery

Tracking No

Status

☐ Started   ☐ Finished   ☐ Delivered

Order Form

ORDER NO:

DATE:

ORDER NAME:

✓

Customer Details

Name :

Address:

Company:

Phone:

Email :

Order Details

#	Item/Description	Qty	Price	Discount	Total
☐					
☐					
☐					
☐					
☐					
☐					
☐					
☐					
☐					
☐					

TOTAL

Payment Details

Subtotal :

Delivery :

Discount :

TAX :

Date

Total

Status

☐ Paid ☐ Half Paid ☐ Pending

Payment Method

☐ Cash ☐ Credit Card ☐ Bank ☐ PayPal

☐ Other :

Delivery Details

Delivery Date :

Method : ☐ Pick-up ☐ Delivery

Tracking No

Status

☐ Started ☐ Finished ☐ Delivered

Special Notes

Order Form - Small Orders

Name : _____

Address: _____

Phone: _____ **Email :** _____

ORDER NO: _____ **DATE:** _____

ORDER NAME: _____ ✓

Order Details

	#	Item/Description	Qty	Price	Discount	Total
☐						
☐						
☐						
☐						
☐						

Notes: **TOTAL** ____

Payment Details

Subtotal : _____

Delivery : _____

Discount: _____ **TAX:** _____

Method : _____

Date ____

Total ____

Status
☐ Paid ☐ Half Paid ☐ Pending

Delivery Details

Delivery Date : _____

Method : ☐ Pick-up ☐ Delivery

Tracking No ____

Status
☐ Started ☐ Finished ☐ Delivered

Order Form - Small Orders

Name : _____

Address: _____

Phone: _____ **Email :** _____

ORDER NO: _____ **DATE:** _____

ORDER NAME: _____ ✓

Order Details

	#	Item/Description	Qty	Price	Discount	Total
☐						
☐						
☐						
☐						
☐						

Notes: **TOTAL** ____

Payment Details

Subtotal : _____

Delivery : _____

Discount: _____ **TAX:** _____

Method : _____

Date ____

Total ____

Status
☐ Paid ☐ Half Paid ☐ Pending

Delivery Details

Delivery Date : _____

Method : ☐ Pick-up ☐ Delivery

Tracking No ____

Status
☐ Started ☐ Finished ☐ Delivered

Order Form

ORDER NO:

DATE:

ORDER NAME:

✓

Customer Details

Name :

Company:

Phone:

Email :

Address:

Order Details

	#	Item/Description	Qty	Price	Discount	Total
☐						
☐						
☐						
☐						
☐						
☐						
☐						
☐						
☐						
☐						

TOTAL

Payment Details

Subtotal :

Delivery :

Discount :

TAX :

Date

Total

Status

☐ Paid   ☐ Half Paid   ☐ Pending

Payment Method

☐ Cash   ☐ Credit Card   ☐ Bank   ☐ PayPal

☐ Other :

Special Notes

Delivery Details

Delivery Date :

Method : ☐ Pick-up   ☐ Delivery

Tracking No

Status

☐ Started   ☐ Finished   ☐ Delivered

Order Form

ORDER NO:

DATE:

ORDER NAME:

✓

Customer Details

Name :

Company:

Phone: Email :

Address:

Order Details

#	Item/Description	Qty	Price	Discount	Total
☐					
☐					
☐					
☐					
☐					
☐					
☐					
☐					
☐					
☐					

TOTAL

Payment Details

Subtotal :

Delivery :

Discount :

TAX   :

Date

Total

Status
☐ Paid ☐ Half Paid ☐ Pending

Payment Method
☐ Cash ☐ Credit Card ☐ Bank ☐ PayPal
☐ Other :

Delivery Details

Delivery Date :

Method   : ☐ Pick-up ☐ Delivery

Tracking No

Status
☐ Started ☐ Finished ☐ Delivered

Special Notes

Order Form

ORDER NO:

DATE:

ORDER NAME:

✓

Customer Details

Name :

Company:

Phone:

Email :

Address:

Order Details

	#	Item/Description	Qty	Price	Discount	Total
☐						
☐						
☐						
☐						
☐						
☐						
☐						
☐						
☐						
☐						

TOTAL

Payment Details

Subtotal :

Delivery :

Discount:

TAX   :

Date

Total

Status

☐ Paid   ☐ Half Paid   ☐ Pending

Payment Method

☐ Cash   ☐ Credit Card   ☐ Bank   ☐ PayPal

☐ Other :

Special Notes

Delivery Details

Delivery Date :

Method   :   ☐ Pick-up   ☐ Delivery

Tracking No

Status

☐ Started   ☐ Finished   ☐ Delivered

Order Form - Small Orders

Name :

Address:

Phone:　　　　　　　**Email :**

ORDER NO:

DATE:

ORDER NAME:　　　　　　　　　　✓

Order Details

#	Item/Description	Qty	Price	Discount	Total
☐					
☐					
☐					
☐					
☐					

Notes:　　　　　　　　　　　　　　　　　**TOTAL**

Payment Details

Subtotal :

Delivery :

Discount:　　**TAX:**

Method　:

Date

Total

Status
☐ Paid　☐ Half Paid　☐ Pending

Delivery Details

Delivery Date :

Method　　　:　☐ Pick-up　☐ Delivery

Tracking No

Status
☐ Started　☐ Finished　☐ Delivered

Order Form - Small Orders

Name :

Address:

Phone:　　　　　　　**Email :**

ORDER NO:

DATE:

ORDER NAME:　　　　　　　　　　✓

Order Details

#	Item/Description	Qty	Price	Discount	Total
☐					
☐					
☐					
☐					
☐					

Notes:　　　　　　　　　　　　　　　　　**TOTAL**

Payment Details

Subtotal :

Delivery :

Discount:　　**TAX:**

Method　:

Date

Total

Status
☐ Paid　☐ Half Paid　☐ Pending

Delivery Details

Delivery Date :

Method　　　:　☐ Pick-up　☐ Delivery

Tracking No

Status
☐ Started　☐ Finished　☐ Delivered

Order Form

ORDER NO:

DATE:

ORDER NAME:

✓

Customer Details

Name :

Address:

Company:

Phone:

Email :

Order Details

☐	#	Item/Description	Qty	Price	Discount	Total
☐						
☐						
☐						
☐						
☐						
☐						
☐						
☐						
☐						
☐						

TOTAL

Payment Details

Subtotal :

Delivery :

Discount:

TAX :

Date

Total

Status
☐ Paid ☐ Half Paid ☐ Pending

Payment Method
☐ Cash ☐ Credit Card ☐ Bank ☐ PayPal
☐ Other :

Special Notes

Delivery Details

Delivery Date :

Method : ☐ Pick-up ☐ Delivery

Tracking No

Status
☐ Started ☐ Finished ☐ Delivered

Order Form

ORDER NO:

DATE:

ORDER NAME:

✓

Customer Details

Name :

Company:

Phone: Email :

Address:

Order Details

	#	Item/Description	Qty	Price	Discount	Total
☐						
☐						
☐						
☐						
☐						
☐						
☐						
☐						
☐						
☐						

TOTAL

Payment Details

Subtotal :

Delivery :

Discount :

TAX   :

Date

Total

Status

☐ Paid   ☐ Half Paid   ☐ Pending

Payment Method

☐ Cash   ☐ Credit Card   ☐ Bank   ☐ PayPal

☐ Other :

Special Notes

Delivery Details

Delivery Date :

Method   :   ☐ Pick-up   ☐ Delivery

Tracking No

Status

☐ Started   ☐ Finished   ☐ Delivered

Order Form

ORDER NO:

DATE:

ORDER NAME:

✓

Customer Details

Name :

Address:

Company:

Phone:

Email :

Order Details

☐	#	Item/Description	Qty	Price	Discount	Total
☐						
☐						
☐						
☐						
☐						
☐						
☐						
☐						
☐						
☐						

TOTAL

Payment Details

Subtotal :

Delivery :

Discount:

TAX :

Date

Total

Status

☐ Paid   ☐ Half Paid   ☐ Pending

Payment Method

☐ Cash   ☐ Credit Card   ☐ Bank   ☐ PayPal

☐ Other :

Delivery Details

Delivery Date :

Method : ☐ Pick-up   ☐ Delivery

Tracking No

Status

☐ Started   ☐ Finished   ☐ Delivered

Special Notes

Order Form - Small Orders

Name : _____

Address: _____

Phone: _____ **Email :** _____

ORDER NO: [_____]

DATE: [_____]

ORDER NAME: [_____] ✓ [ ]

Order Details

#	Item/Description	Qty	Price	Discount	Total
[ ]					
[ ]					
[ ]					
[ ]					
[ ]					

Notes:

TOTAL [_____]

Payment Details

Subtotal : _____

Delivery : _____

Discount: _____ **TAX:** _____

Method : _____

Date [_____]

Total [_____]

Status
[ ] Paid [ ] Half Paid [ ] Pending

Delivery Details

Delivery Date : _____

Method : [ ] Pick-up [ ] Delivery

Tracking No [_____]

Status
[ ] Started [ ] Finished [ ] Delivered

Order Form - Small Orders

Name : _____

Address: _____

Phone: _____ **Email :** _____

ORDER NO: [_____]

DATE: [_____]

ORDER NAME: [_____] ✓ [ ]

Order Details

#	Item/Description	Qty	Price	Discount	Total
[ ]					
[ ]					
[ ]					
[ ]					
[ ]					

Notes:

TOTAL [_____]

Payment Details

Subtotal : _____

Delivery : _____

Discount: _____ **TAX:** _____

Method : _____

Date [_____]

Total [_____]

Status
[ ] Paid [ ] Half Paid [ ] Pending

Delivery Details

Delivery Date : _____

Method : [ ] Pick-up [ ] Delivery

Tracking No [_____]

Status
[ ] Started [ ] Finished [ ] Delivered

Order Form

ORDER NO:

DATE:

ORDER NAME:

✓

Customer Details

Name :

Address:

Company:

Phone:

Email :

Order Details

	#	Item/Description	Qty	Price	Discount	Total
☐						
☐						
☐						
☐						
☐						
☐						
☐						
☐						
☐						
☐						

TOTAL

Payment Details

Subtotal :

Delivery :

Discount:

TAX :

Date

Total

Status
☐ Paid ☐ Half Paid ☐ Pending

Payment Method
☐ Cash ☐ Credit Card ☐ Bank ☐ PayPal
☐ Other :

Special Notes

Delivery Details

Delivery Date :

Method : ☐ Pick-up ☐ Delivery

Tracking No

Status
☐ Started ☐ Finished ☐ Delivered

Order Form

ORDER NO:

DATE:

ORDER NAME:

✓

Customer Details

Name :

Company:

Phone: Email :

Address:

Order Details

	#	Item/Description	Qty	Price	Discount	Total
☐						
☐						
☐						
☐						
☐						
☐						
☐						
☐						
☐						
☐						

TOTAL

Payment Details

Subtotal :

Delivery :

Discount :

TAX   :

Date

Total

Status
☐ Paid   ☐ Half Paid   ☐ Pending

Payment Method
☐ Cash   ☐ Credit Card   ☐ Bank   ☐ PayPal
☐ Other :

Delivery Details

Delivery Date :

Method   :   ☐ Pick-up   ☐ Delivery

Tracking No

Status
☐ Started   ☐ Finished   ☐ Delivered

Special Notes

Order Form

ORDER NO:

DATE:

ORDER NAME:

✓

Customer Details

Name :

Address:

Company:

Phone:

Email :

Order Details

#	Item/Description	Qty	Price	Discount	Total
☐					
☐					
☐					
☐					
☐					
☐					
☐					
☐					
☐					
☐					

TOTAL

Payment Details

Subtotal :

Delivery :

Discount:

TAX   :

Date

Total

Status

☐ Paid   ☐ Half Paid   ☐ Pending

Payment Method

☐ Cash   ☐ Credit Card   ☐ Bank   ☐ PayPal

☐ Other :

Delivery Details

Delivery Date :

Method   :   ☐ Pick-up   ☐ Delivery

Tracking No

Status

☐ Started   ☐ Finished   ☐ Delivered

Special Notes

Order Form - Small Orders

Name :

Address:

Phone: **Email :**

ORDER NO:

DATE:

ORDER NAME: ✓

Order Details

	#	Item/Description	Qty	Price	Discount	Total
☐						
☐						
☐						
☐						
☐						

Notes: **TOTAL**

Payment Details

Subtotal :

Delivery :

Discount: **TAX:**

Method :

Date

Total

Status
☐ Paid ☐ Half Paid ☐ Pending

Delivery Details

Delivery Date :

Method : ☐ Pick-up ☐ Delivery

Tracking No

Status
☐ Started ☐ Finished ☐ Delivered

Order Form - Small Orders

Name :

Address:

Phone: **Email :**

ORDER NO:

DATE:

ORDER NAME: ✓

Order Details

	#	Item/Description	Qty	Price	Discount	Total
☐						
☐						
☐						
☐						
☐						

Notes: **TOTAL**

Payment Details

Subtotal :

Delivery :

Discount: **TAX:**

Method :

Date

Total

Status
☐ Paid ☐ Half Paid ☐ Pending

Delivery Details

Delivery Date :

Method : ☐ Pick-up ☐ Delivery

Tracking No

Status
☐ Started ☐ Finished ☐ Delivered

Order Form

ORDER NO:

DATE:

ORDER NAME:

✓

Customer Details

Name :

Address:

Company:

Phone: Email :

Order Details

#	Item/Description	Qty	Price	Discount	Total
☐					
☐					
☐					
☐					
☐					
☐					
☐					
☐					
☐					
☐					

TOTAL

Payment Details

Subtotal :

Delivery :

Discount :

TAX   :

Date

Total

Status

☐ Paid   ☐ Half Paid   ☐ Pending

Payment Method

☐ Cash   ☐ Credit Card   ☐ Bank   ☐ PayPal

☐ Other :

Delivery Details

Delivery Date :

Method   :   ☐ Pick-up   ☐ Delivery

Tracking No

Status

☐ Started   ☐ Finished   ☐ Delivered

Special Notes

Order Form

ORDER NO:

DATE:

ORDER NAME:

✓

Customer Details

Name :

Address:

Company:

Phone:

Email :

Order Details

#	Item/Description	Qty	Price	Discount	Total
☐					
☐					
☐					
☐					
☐					
☐					
☐					
☐					
☐					
☐					

TOTAL

Payment Details

Subtotal :

Delivery :

Discount :

TAX :

Date

Total

Status

☐ Paid   ☐ Half Paid   ☐ Pending

Payment Method

☐ Cash   ☐ Credit Card   ☐ Bank   ☐ PayPal

☐ Other :

Delivery Details

Delivery Date :

Method : ☐ Pick-up   ☐ Delivery

Tracking No

Status

☐ Started   ☐ Finished   ☐ Delivered

Special Notes

Order Form

ORDER NO:

DATE:

ORDER NAME:

✓

Customer Details

Name :

Company:

Phone: Email :

Address:

Order Details

	#	Item/Description	Qty	Price	Discount	Total
☐						
☐						
☐						
☐						
☐						
☐						
☐						
☐						
☐						
☐						
					TOTAL	

Payment Details

Subtotal :

Delivery :

Discount :

TAX   :

Date

Total

Status
☐ Paid   ☐ Half Paid   ☐ Pending

Payment Method
☐ Cash   ☐ Credit Card   ☐ Bank   ☐ PayPal
☐ Other :

Special Notes

Delivery Details

Delivery Date :

Method   :   ☐ Pick-up   ☐ Delivery

Tracking No

Status
☐ Started   ☐ Finished   ☐ Delivered

Order Form - Small Orders

Name :

Address:

Phone: **Email :**

ORDER NO:

DATE:

ORDER NAME: ✓

Order Details

	#	Item/Description	Qty	Price	Discount	Total
☐						
☐						
☐						
☐						
☐						

Notes: **TOTAL**

Payment Details

Subtotal :

Delivery :

Discount: **TAX:**

Method :

Date

Total

Status
☐ Paid   ☐ Half Paid   ☐ Pending

Delivery Details

Delivery Date :

Method   : ☐ Pick-up   ☐ Delivery

Tracking No

Status
☐ Started   ☐ Finished   ☐ Delivered

Order Form - Small Orders

Name :

Address:

Phone: **Email :**

ORDER NO:

DATE:

ORDER NAME: ✓

Order Details

	#	Item/Description	Qty	Price	Discount	Total
☐						
☐						
☐						
☐						
☐						

Notes: **TOTAL**

Payment Details

Subtotal :

Delivery :

Discount: **TAX:**

Method :

Date

Total

Status
☐ Paid   ☐ Half Paid   ☐ Pending

Delivery Details

Delivery Date :

Method   : ☐ Pick-up   ☐ Delivery

Tracking No

Status
☐ Started   ☐ Finished   ☐ Delivered

Order Form

ORDER NO:

DATE:

ORDER NAME:

✓

Customer Details

Name :

Company:

Phone: Email :

Address:

Order Details

	#	Item/Description	Qty	Price	Discount	Total
☐						
☐						
☐						
☐						
☐						
☐						
☐						
☐						
☐						
☐						
					TOTAL	

Payment Details

Subtotal :

Delivery :

Discount:

TAX   :

Date

Total

Status

☐ Paid   ☐ Half Paid   ☐ Pending

Payment Method

☐ Cash   ☐ Credit Card   ☐ Bank   ☐ PayPal

☐ Other :

Special Notes

Delivery Details

Delivery Date :

Method   :   ☐ Pick-up   ☐ Delivery

Tracking No

Status

☐ Started   ☐ Finished   ☐ Delivered

Order Form

ORDER NO: _____

DATE: _____

ORDER NAME: _____

✓ ☐

Customer Details

Name : _____

Address: _____

Company: _____

_____

Phone: _____

Email : _____

_____

Order Details

☐	#	Item/Description	Qty	Price	Discount	Total
☐						
☐						
☐						
☐						
☐						
☐						
☐						
☐						
☐						
☐						

TOTAL _____

Payment Details

Subtotal : _____

Delivery : _____

Discount : _____

TAX : _____

Date _____

Total _____

Status

☐ Paid   ☐ Half Paid   ☐ Pending

Payment Method

☐ Cash   ☐ Credit Card   ☐ Bank   ☐ PayPal

☐ Other : _____

Delivery Details

Delivery Date : _____

Method : ☐ Pick-up   ☐ Delivery

Tracking No

Status

☐ Started   ☐ Finished   ☐ Delivered

Special Notes

Order Form

ORDER NO:

DATE:

ORDER NAME:

✓

Customer Details

Name :

Company:

Phone:

Email :

Address:

Order Details

#	Item/Description	Qty	Price	Discount	Total
☐					
☐					
☐					
☐					
☐					
☐					
☐					
☐					
☐					
☐					

TOTAL

Payment Details

Subtotal :

Delivery :

Discount :

TAX :

Date

Total

Status

☐ Paid   ☐ Half Paid   ☐ Pending

Payment Method

☐ Cash   ☐ Credit Card   ☐ Bank   ☐ PayPal

☐ Other :

Delivery Details

Delivery Date :

Method : ☐ Pick-up   ☐ Delivery

Tracking No

Status

☐ Started   ☐ Finished   ☐ Delivered

Special Notes

Order Form - Small Orders

Name :

Address:

Phone: **Email :**

ORDER NO:

DATE:

ORDER NAME: ✓

Order Details

#	Item/Description	Qty	Price	Discount	Total
☐					
☐					
☐					
☐					
☐					

Notes: **TOTAL**

Payment Details

Subtotal :

Delivery :

Discount: **TAX:**

Method :

Date

Total

Status
☐ Paid ☐ Half Paid ☐ Pending

Delivery Details

Delivery Date :

Method   : ☐ Pick-up ☐ Delivery

Tracking No

Status
☐ Started ☐ Finished ☐ Delivered

Order Form - Small Orders

Name :

Address:

Phone: **Email :**

ORDER NO:

DATE:

ORDER NAME: ✓

Order Details

#	Item/Description	Qty	Price	Discount	Total
☐					
☐					
☐					
☐					
☐					

Notes: **TOTAL**

Payment Details

Subtotal :

Delivery :

Discount: **TAX:**

Method :

Date

Total

Status
☐ Paid ☐ Half Paid ☐ Pending

Delivery Details

Delivery Date :

Method   : ☐ Pick-up ☐ Delivery

Tracking No

Status
☐ Started ☐ Finished ☐ Delivered

Order Form

ORDER NO:

DATE:

ORDER NAME:

✓

Customer Details

Name :

Company:

Phone: Email :

Address:

Order Details

#	Item/Description	Qty	Price	Discount	Total
☐					
☐					
☐					
☐					
☐					
☐					
☐					
☐					
☐					
☐					

TOTAL

Payment Details

Subtotal :

Delivery :

Discount:

TAX   :

Date

Total

Status

☐ Paid   ☐ Half Paid   ☐ Pending

Payment Method

☐ Cash   ☐ Credit Card   ☐ Bank   ☐ PayPal

☐ Other :

Delivery Details

Delivery Date :

Method   :   ☐ Pick-up   ☐ Delivery

Tracking No

Status

☐ Started   ☐ Finished   ☐ Delivered

Special Notes

Order Form

ORDER NO:

DATE:

ORDER NAME:

✓

Customer Details

Name :

Address:

Company:

Phone:

Email :

Order Details

	#	Item/Description	Qty	Price	Discount	Total
☐						
☐						
☐						
☐						
☐						
☐						
☐						
☐						
☐						
☐						

TOTAL

Payment Details

Subtotal :

Delivery :

Discount :

TAX :

Date

Total

Status
☐ Paid ☐ Half Paid ☐ Pending

Payment Method
☐ Cash ☐ Credit Card ☐ Bank ☐ PayPal
☐ Other :

Special Notes

Delivery Details

Delivery Date :

Method : ☐ Pick-up ☐ Delivery

Tracking No

Status
☐ Started ☐ Finished ☐ Delivered

Order Form

ORDER NO:

DATE:

ORDER NAME:

✓

Customer Details

Name :

Address:

Company:

Phone:

Email :

Order Details

	#	Item/Description	Qty	Price	Discount	Total
☐						
☐						
☐						
☐						
☐						
☐						
☐						
☐						
☐						
☐						

TOTAL

Payment Details

Subtotal :

Delivery :

Discount :

TAX :

Date

Total

Status

☐ Paid   ☐ Half Paid   ☐ Pending

Payment Method

☐ Cash   ☐ Credit Card   ☐ Bank   ☐ PayPal

☐ Other :

Delivery Details

Delivery Date :

Method : ☐ Pick-up   ☐ Delivery

Tracking No

Status

☐ Started   ☐ Finished   ☐ Delivered

Special Notes

Order Form - Small Orders

Name :

Address:

Phone: **Email :**

ORDER NO:

DATE:

ORDER NAME: ✓

Order Details

#	Item/Description	Qty	Price	Discount	Total
☐					
☐					
☐					
☐					
☐					

Notes: **TOTAL**

Payment Details

Subtotal :

Delivery :

Discount: **TAX:**

Method :

Date

Total

Status
☐ Paid   ☐ Half Paid   ☐ Pending

Delivery Details

Delivery Date :

Method   : ☐ Pick-up   ☐ Delivery

Tracking No

Status
☐ Started   ☐ Finished   ☐ Delivered

Order Form - Small Orders

Name :

Address:

Phone: **Email :**

ORDER NO:

DATE:

ORDER NAME: ✓

Order Details

#	Item/Description	Qty	Price	Discount	Total
☐					
☐					
☐					
☐					
☐					

Notes: **TOTAL**

Payment Details

Subtotal :

Delivery :

Discount: **TAX:**

Method :

Date

Total

Status
☐ Paid   ☐ Half Paid   ☐ Pending

Delivery Details

Delivery Date :

Method   : ☐ Pick-up   ☐ Delivery

Tracking No

Status
☐ Started   ☐ Finished   ☐ Delivered

Order Form

ORDER NO:

DATE:

ORDER NAME:

✓

Customer Details

Name :

Company:

Phone: Email :

Address:

Order Details

#	Item/Description	Qty	Price	Discount	Total
☐					
☐					
☐					
☐					
☐					
☐					
☐					
☐					
☐					
☐					

TOTAL

Payment Details

Subtotal :

Delivery :

Discount :

TAX   :

Date

Total

Status
☐ Paid   ☐ Half Paid   ☐ Pending

Payment Method
☐ Cash   ☐ Credit Card   ☐ Bank   ☐ PayPal
☐ Other :

Delivery Details

Delivery Date :

Method   :   ☐ Pick-up   ☐ Delivery

Tracking No

Status
☐ Started   ☐ Finished   ☐ Delivered

Special Notes

Order Form

ORDER NO:

DATE:

ORDER NAME:

✓

Customer Details

Name :

Company:

Phone:

Email :

Address:

Order Details

#	Item/Description	Qty	Price	Discount	Total
☐					
☐					
☐					
☐					
☐					
☐					
☐					
☐					
☐					
☐					

TOTAL

Payment Details

Subtotal :

Delivery :

Discount :

TAX   :

Date

Total

Status
☐ Paid ☐ Half Paid ☐ Pending

Payment Method

☐ Cash ☐ Credit Card ☐ Bank ☐ PayPal

☐ Other :

Delivery Details

Delivery Date :

Method   : ☐ Pick-up ☐ Delivery

Tracking No

Status
☐ Started ☐ Finished ☐ Delivered

Special Notes

Order Form

ORDER NO:

DATE:

ORDER NAME:

✓

Customer Details

Name :

Company:

Phone: Email :

Address:

Order Details

☐	#	Item/Description	Qty	Price	Discount	Total
☐						
☐						
☐						
☐						
☐						
☐						
☐						
☐						
☐						
☐						

TOTAL

Payment Details

Subtotal :

Delivery :

Discount :

TAX   :

Date

Total

Status
☐ Paid   ☐ Half Paid   ☐ Pending

Payment Method
☐ Cash   ☐ Credit Card   ☐ Bank   ☐ PayPal
☐ Other :

Delivery Details

Delivery Date :

Method   :   ☐ Pick-up   ☐ Delivery

Tracking No

Status
☐ Started   ☐ Finished   ☐ Delivered

Special Notes

Order Form - Small Orders

ORDER NO:

DATE:

Name :

Address:

Phone: Email :

ORDER NAME: ✓

Order Details

#	Item/Description	Qty	Price	Discount	Total
☐					
☐					
☐					
☐					
☐					

Notes: **TOTAL**

Payment Details

Subtotal :

Delivery :

Discount: TAX:

Method :

Date

Total

Status
☐ Paid   ☐ Half Paid   ☐ Pending

Delivery Details

Delivery Date :

Method   :   ☐ Pick-up   ☐ Delivery

Tracking No

Status
☐ Started   ☐ Finished   ☐ Delivered

Order Form - Small Orders

ORDER NO:

DATE:

Name :

Address:

Phone: Email :

ORDER NAME: ✓

Order Details

#	Item/Description	Qty	Price	Discount	Total
☐					
☐					
☐					
☐					
☐					

Notes: **TOTAL**

Payment Details

Subtotal :

Delivery :

Discount: TAX:

Method :

Date

Total

Status
☐ Paid   ☐ Half Paid   ☐ Pending

Delivery Details

Delivery Date :

Method   :   ☐ Pick-up   ☐ Delivery

Tracking No

Status
☐ Started   ☐ Finished   ☐ Delivered

Order Form

ORDER NO:

DATE:

ORDER NAME:

✓

Customer Details

Name :

Company:

Phone:

Email :

Address:

Order Details

	#	Item/Description	Qty	Price	Discount	Total
☐						
☐						
☐						
☐						
☐						
☐						
☐						
☐						
☐						
☐						

TOTAL

Payment Details

Subtotal :

Delivery :

Discount:

TAX :

Date

Total

Status

☐ Paid ☐ Half Paid ☐ Pending

Payment Method

☐ Cash ☐ Credit Card ☐ Bank ☐ PayPal

☐ Other :

Special Notes

Delivery Details

Delivery Date :

Method : ☐ Pick-up ☐ Delivery

Tracking No

Status

☐ Started ☐ Finished ☐ Delivered

Order Form

ORDER NO:

DATE:

ORDER NAME:

✓

Customer Details

Name :

Company:

Phone:

Email :

Address:

Order Details

#	Item/Description	Qty	Price	Discount	Total
☐					
☐					
☐					
☐					
☐					
☐					
☐					
☐					
☐					
☐					

TOTAL

Payment Details

Subtotal :

Delivery :

Discount :

TAX :

Date

Total

Status

☐ Paid   ☐ Half Paid   ☐ Pending

Payment Method

☐ Cash   ☐ Credit Card   ☐ Bank   ☐ PayPal

☐ Other :

Special Notes

Delivery Details

Delivery Date :

Method : ☐ Pick-up   ☐ Delivery

Tracking No

Status

☐ Started   ☐ Finished   ☐ Delivered

Order Form

ORDER NO:

DATE:

ORDER NAME:

✓

Customer Details

Name :

Company:

Phone:

Email :

Address:

Order Details

#	Item/Description	Qty	Price	Discount	Total
☐					
☐					
☐					
☐					
☐					
☐					
☐					
☐					
☐					
☐					
				TOTAL	

Payment Details

Subtotal :

Delivery :

Discount:

TAX :

Date

Total

Status

☐ Paid ☐ Half Paid ☐ Pending

Payment Method

☐ Cash ☐ Credit Card ☐ Bank ☐ PayPal

☐ Other :

Special Notes

Delivery Details

Delivery Date :

Method : ☐ Pick-up ☐ Delivery

Tracking No

Status

☐ Started ☐ Finished ☐ Delivered

Order Form - Small Orders

Name :

Address:

Phone: **Email :**

ORDER NO:

DATE:

ORDER NAME: ✓

Order Details

	#	Item/Description	Qty	Price	Discount	Total
☐						
☐						
☐						
☐						
☐						

Notes: **TOTAL**

Payment Details

Subtotal :

Delivery :

Discount: **TAX:**

Method :

Date

Total

Status
☐ Paid   ☐ Half Paid   ☐ Pending

Delivery Details

Delivery Date :

Method   : ☐ Pick-up   ☐ Delivery

Tracking No

Status
☐ Started   ☐ Finished   ☐ Delivered

Order Form - Small Orders

Name :

Address:

Phone: **Email :**

ORDER NO:

DATE:

ORDER NAME: ✓

Order Details

	#	Item/Description	Qty	Price	Discount	Total
☐						
☐						
☐						
☐						
☐						

Notes: **TOTAL**

Payment Details

Subtotal :

Delivery :

Discount: **TAX:**

Method :

Date

Total

Status
☐ Paid   ☐ Half Paid   ☐ Pending

Delivery Details

Delivery Date :

Method   : ☐ Pick-up   ☐ Delivery

Tracking No

Status
☐ Started   ☐ Finished   ☐ Delivered

Order Form

ORDER NO:

DATE:

ORDER NAME:

✓

Customer Details

Name :

Address:

Company:

Phone:

Email :

Order Details

#	Item/Description	Qty	Price	Discount	Total
☐					
☐					
☐					
☐					
☐					
☐					
☐					
☐					
☐					
☐					

TOTAL

Payment Details

Subtotal :

Delivery :

Discount :

TAX   :

Date

Total

Status
☐ Paid   ☐ Half Paid   ☐ Pending

Payment Method
☐ Cash ☐ Credit Card ☐ Bank ☐ PayPal
☐ Other :

Delivery Details

Delivery Date :

Method   :   ☐ Pick-up   ☐ Delivery

Tracking No

Status
☐ Started   ☐ Finished   ☐ Delivered

Special Notes

Order Form

ORDER NO:

DATE:

ORDER NAME:

✓

Customer Details

Name :

Address:

Company:

Phone:

Email :

Order Details

#	Item/Description	Qty	Price	Discount	Total
☐					
☐					
☐					
☐					
☐					
☐					
☐					
☐					
☐					
☐					
				TOTAL	

Payment Details

Subtotal :

Delivery :

Discount :

TAX   :

Date

Total

Status

☐ Paid   ☐ Half Paid   ☐ Pending

Payment Method

☐ Cash   ☐ Credit Card   ☐ Bank   ☐ PayPal

☐ Other :

Special Notes

Delivery Details

Delivery Date :

Method   :   ☐ Pick-up   ☐ Delivery

Tracking No

Status

☐ Started   ☐ Finished   ☐ Delivered

Order Form

ORDER NO:

DATE:

ORDER NAME:

✓

Customer Details

Name :

Company:

Phone:

Email :

Address:

Order Details

	#	Item/Description	Qty	Price	Discount	Total
☐						
☐						
☐						
☐						
☐						
☐						
☐						
☐						
☐						
☐						

TOTAL

Payment Details

Subtotal :

Delivery :

Discount:

TAX :

Date

Total

Status

☐ Paid   ☐ Half Paid   ☐ Pending

Payment Method

☐ Cash   ☐ Credit Card   ☐ Bank   ☐ PayPal

☐ Other :

Special Notes

Delivery Details

Delivery Date :

Method : ☐ Pick-up   ☐ Delivery

Tracking No

Status

☐ Started   ☐ Finished   ☐ Delivered

Order Form - Small Orders

Name :

Address:

Phone: Email :

ORDER NO:

DATE:

ORDER NAME: ✓

Order Details

#	Item/Description	Qty	Price	Discount	Total
☐					
☐					
☐					
☐					
☐					

Notes: **TOTAL**

Payment Details

Subtotal :

Delivery :

Discount: TAX:

Method :

Date

Total

Status
☐ Paid   ☐ Half Paid   ☐ Pending

Delivery Details

Delivery Date :

Method   :   ☐ Pick-up   ☐ Delivery

Tracking No

Status
☐ Started   ☐ Finished   ☐ Delivered

Order Form - Small Orders

Name :

Address:

Phone: Email :

ORDER NO:

DATE:

ORDER NAME: ✓

Order Details

#	Item/Description	Qty	Price	Discount	Total
☐					
☐					
☐					
☐					
☐					

Notes: **TOTAL**

Payment Details

Subtotal :

Delivery :

Discount: TAX:

Method :

Date

Total

Status
☐ Paid   ☐ Half Paid   ☐ Pending

Delivery Details

Delivery Date :

Method   :   ☐ Pick-up   ☐ Delivery

Tracking No

Status
☐ Started   ☐ Finished   ☐ Delivered

Order Form

ORDER NO:

DATE:

ORDER NAME:

✓

Customer Details

Name :

Address:

Company:

Phone:

Email :

Order Details

	#	Item/Description	Qty	Price	Discount	Total
☐						
☐						
☐						
☐						
☐						
☐						
☐						
☐						
☐						
☐						
					TOTAL	

Payment Details

Subtotal :

Delivery :

Discount:

TAX :

Date

Total

Status

☐ Paid ☐ Half Paid ☐ Pending

Payment Method

☐ Cash ☐ Credit Card ☐ Bank ☐ PayPal

☐ Other :

Delivery Details

Delivery Date :

Method : ☐ Pick-up ☐ Delivery

Tracking No

Status

☐ Started ☐ Finished ☐ Delivered

Special Notes

Order Form

ORDER NO:

DATE:

ORDER NAME:

√

Customer Details

Name :

Company:

Phone:

Email :

Address:

Order Details

	#	Item/Description	Qty	Price	Discount	Total
☐						
☐						
☐						
☐						
☐						
☐						
☐						
☐						
☐						
☐						

TOTAL

Payment Details

Subtotal :

Delivery :

Discount :

TAX :

Date

Total

Status

☐ Paid ☐ Half Paid ☐ Pending

Payment Method

☐ Cash ☐ Credit Card ☐ Bank ☐ PayPal

☐ Other :

Delivery Details

Delivery Date :

Method : ☐ Pick-up ☐ Delivery

Tracking No

Status

☐ Started ☐ Finished ☐ Delivered

Special Notes

Order Form

ORDER NO:

DATE:

ORDER NAME:

✓

Customer Details

Name :

Address:

Company:

Phone: Email :

Order Details

#	Item/Description	Qty	Price	Discount	Total
☐					
☐					
☐					
☐					
☐					
☐					
☐					
☐					
☐					
☐					
				TOTAL	

Payment Details

Subtotal :

Delivery :

Discount :

TAX   :

Date

Total

Status

☐ Paid   ☐ Half Paid   ☐ Pending

Payment Method

☐ Cash   ☐ Credit Card   ☐ Bank   ☐ PayPal

☐ Other :

Special Notes

Delivery Details

Delivery Date :

Method   :   ☐ Pick-up   ☐ Delivery

Tracking No

Status

☐ Started   ☐ Finished   ☐ Delivered

Order Form - Small Orders

Name :

Address:

Phone: **Email :**

ORDER NO:

DATE:

ORDER NAME: ✓

Order Details

#	Item/Description	Qty	Price	Discount	Total
☐					
☐					
☐					
☐					
☐					

Notes: **TOTAL**

Payment Details

Subtotal :

Delivery :

Discount: **TAX:**

Method :

Date

Total

Status
☐ Paid   ☐ Half Paid   ☐ Pending

Delivery Details

Delivery Date :

Method   : ☐ Pick-up ☐ Delivery

Tracking No

Status
☐ Started   ☐ Finished   ☐ Delivered

Order Form - Small Orders

Name :

Address:

Phone: **Email :**

ORDER NO:

DATE:

ORDER NAME: ✓

Order Details

#	Item/Description	Qty	Price	Discount	Total
☐					
☐					
☐					
☐					
☐					

Notes: **TOTAL**

Payment Details

Subtotal :

Delivery :

Discount: **TAX:**

Method :

Date

Total

Status
☐ Paid   ☐ Half Paid   ☐ Pending

Delivery Details

Delivery Date :

Method   : ☐ Pick-up ☐ Delivery

Tracking No

Status
☐ Started   ☐ Finished   ☐ Delivered

Order Form

ORDER NO:

DATE:

ORDER NAME:

✓

Customer Details

Name :

Address:

Company:

Phone:

Email :

Order Details

	#	Item/Description	Qty	Price	Discount	Total
☐						
☐						
☐						
☐						
☐						
☐						
☐						
☐						
☐						
☐						

TOTAL

Payment Details

Subtotal :

Delivery :

Discount :

TAX :

Date

Total

Status

☐ Paid   ☐ Half Paid   ☐ Pending

Payment Method

☐ Cash   ☐ Credit Card   ☐ Bank   ☐ PayPal

☐ Other :

Special Notes

Delivery Details

Delivery Date :

Method : ☐ Pick-up   ☐ Delivery

Tracking No

Status

☐ Started   ☐ Finished   ☐ Delivered

Order Form

ORDER NO: _____

DATE: _____

ORDER NAME: _____

✓ ☐

Customer Details

Name : _____

Company: _____

Phone: _____ Email : _____

Address: _____

_____

_____

Order Details

☐	#	Item/Description	Qty	Price	Discount	Total
☐						
☐						
☐						
☐						
☐						
☐						
☐						
☐						
☐						
☐						
					TOTAL	

Payment Details

Subtotal : _____

Delivery : _____

Discount : _____

TAX   : _____

Date

Total

Status

☐ Paid   ☐ Half Paid   ☐ Pending

Payment Method

☐ Cash ☐ Credit Card ☐ Bank ☐ PayPal

☐ Other : _____

Delivery Details

Delivery Date : _____

Method   : ☐ Pick-up ☐ Delivery

Tracking No

Status

☐ Started ☐ Finished ☐ Delivered

Special Notes

Order Form

ORDER NO:

DATE:

ORDER NAME:

✓

Customer Details

Name :

Company:

Phone: Email :

Address:

Order Details

#	Item/Description	Qty	Price	Discount	Total
☐					
☐					
☐					
☐					
☐					
☐					
☐					
☐					
☐					
☐					

TOTAL

Payment Details

Subtotal :

Delivery :

Discount:

TAX   :

Date

Total

Status

☐ Paid   ☐ Half Paid   ☐ Pending

Payment Method

☐ Cash   ☐ Credit Card   ☐ Bank   ☐ PayPal

☐ Other :

Delivery Details

Delivery Date :

Method   :   ☐ Pick-up   ☐ Delivery

Tracking No

Status

☐ Started   ☐ Finished   ☐ Delivered

Special Notes

Order Form - Small Orders

Name : _____

Address: _____

Phone: _____ **Email :** _____

ORDER NO: _____

DATE: _____

ORDER NAME: _____ ✓

Order Details

	#	Item/Description	Qty	Price	Discount	Total
☐						
☐						
☐						
☐						
☐						

Notes: **TOTAL** [ ]

Payment Details

Subtotal : _____

Delivery : _____

Discount: _____ **TAX:** _____

Method : _____

Date [ ]

Total [ ]

Status
☐ Paid   ☐ Half Paid   ☐ Pending

Delivery Details

Delivery Date : _____

Method : ☐ Pick-up ☐ Delivery

Tracking No _____

Status
☐ Started   ☐ Finished   ☐ Delivered

Order Form - Small Orders

Name : _____

Address: _____

Phone: _____ **Email :** _____

ORDER NO: _____

DATE: _____

ORDER NAME: _____ ✓

Order Details

	#	Item/Description	Qty	Price	Discount	Total
☐						
☐						
☐						
☐						
☐						

Notes: **TOTAL** [ ]

Payment Details

Subtotal : _____

Delivery : _____

Discount: _____ **TAX:** _____

Method : _____

Date [ ]

Total [ ]

Status
☐ Paid   ☐ Half Paid   ☐ Pending

Delivery Details

Delivery Date : _____

Method : ☐ Pick-up ☐ Delivery

Tracking No _____

Status
☐ Started   ☐ Finished   ☐ Delivered

Order Form

ORDER NO:

DATE:

ORDER NAME:

✓

Customer Details

Name :

Address:

Company:

Phone:

Email :

Order Details

	#	Item/Description	Qty	Price	Discount	Total
☐						
☐						
☐						
☐						
☐						
☐						
☐						
☐						
☐						
☐						

TOTAL

Payment Details

Subtotal :

Delivery :

Discount:

TAX   :

Date

Total

Status
☐ Paid   ☐ Half Paid   ☐ Pending

Payment Method
☐ Cash   ☐ Credit Card   ☐ Bank   ☐ PayPal
☐ Other :

Delivery Details

Delivery Date :

Method   :   ☐ Pick-up   ☐ Delivery

Tracking No

Status
☐ Started   ☐ Finished   ☐ Delivered

Special Notes

Order Form

ORDER NO:

DATE:

ORDER NAME:

✓

Customer Details

Name :

Address:

Company:

Phone:

Email :

Order Details

#	Item/Description	Qty	Price	Discount	Total
☐					
☐					
☐					
☐					
☐					
☐					
☐					
☐					
☐					
☐					
				TOTAL	

Payment Details

Subtotal :

Delivery :

Discount :

TAX :

Date

Total

Status

☐ Paid   ☐ Half Paid   ☐ Pending

Payment Method

☐ Cash   ☐ Credit Card   ☐ Bank   ☐ PayPal

☐ Other :

Delivery Details

Delivery Date :

Method : ☐ Pick-up   ☐ Delivery

Tracking No

Status

☐ Started   ☐ Finished   ☐ Delivered

Special Notes

Order Form

ORDER NO:

DATE:

ORDER NAME:

✓

Customer Details

Name :

Company:

Phone: Email :

Address:

Order Details

	#	Item/Description	Qty	Price	Discount	Total
☐						
☐						
☐						
☐						
☐						
☐						
☐						
☐						
☐						
☐						

TOTAL

Payment Details

Subtotal :

Delivery :

Discount :

TAX   :

Date

Total

Status
☐ Paid   ☐ Half Paid   ☐ Pending

Payment Method
☐ Cash   ☐ Credit Card   ☐ Bank   ☐ PayPal
☐ Other :

Delivery Details

Delivery Date :

Method   :   ☐ Pick-up   ☐ Delivery

Tracking No

Status
☐ Started   ☐ Finished   ☐ Delivered

Special Notes

Order Form - Small Orders

ORDER NO:

DATE:

Name :

Address:

Phone: Email :

ORDER NAME: ✓

Order Details

#	Item/Description	Qty	Price	Discount	Total
☐					
☐					
☐					
☐					
☐					

Notes: **TOTAL**

Payment Details

Subtotal :

Delivery :

Discount: TAX:

Method   :

Date

Total

Status

☐ Paid ☐ Half Paid ☐ Pending

Delivery Details

Delivery Date :

Method   : ☐ Pick-up   ☐ Delivery

Tracking No

Status

☐ Started   ☐ Finished   ☐ Delivered

Order Form - Small Orders

ORDER NO:

DATE:

Name :

Address:

Phone: Email :

ORDER NAME: ✓

Order Details

#	Item/Description	Qty	Price	Discount	Total
☐					
☐					
☐					
☐					
☐					

Notes: **TOTAL**

Payment Details

Subtotal :

Delivery :

Discount: TAX:

Method   :

Date

Total

Status

☐ Paid ☐ Half Paid ☐ Pending

Delivery Details

Delivery Date :

Method   : ☐ Pick-up   ☐ Delivery

Tracking No

Status

☐ Started   ☐ Finished   ☐ Delivered

Order Form

ORDER NO: _____

DATE: _____

ORDER NAME: _____ ✓ ☐

Customer Details

Name : _____

Company: _____

Phone: _____ Email : _____

Address: _____

_____

_____

Order Details

☐	#	Item/Description	Qty	Price	Discount	Total
☐						
☐						
☐						
☐						
☐						
☐						
☐						
☐						
☐						
☐						
					TOTAL	

Payment Details

Subtotal : _____

Delivery : _____

Discount: _____

TAX   : _____

Date

Total

Status
☐ Paid ☐ Half Paid ☐ Pending

Payment Method
☐ Cash ☐ Credit Card ☐ Bank ☐ PayPal
☐ Other :

Delivery Details

Delivery Date : _____

Method   : ☐ Pick-up ☐ Delivery

Tracking No

Status
☐ Started ☐ Finished ☐ Delivered

Special Notes

Order Form

ORDER NO:

DATE:

ORDER NAME:

✓

Customer Details

Name :

Company:

Phone:

Email :

Address:

Order Details

☐ #	Item/Description	Qty	Price	Discount	Total
☐					
☐					
☐					
☐					
☐					
☐					
☐					
☐					
☐					
☐					

TOTAL

Payment Details

Subtotal :

Delivery :

Discount :

TAX　　 :

Date

Total

Status
☐ Paid ☐ Half Paid ☐ Pending

Payment Method
☐ Cash ☐ Credit Card ☐ Bank ☐ PayPal
☐ Other :

Special Notes

Delivery Details

Delivery Date :

Method　　　 : ☐ Pick-up ☐ Delivery

Tracking No

Status
☐ Started ☐ Finished ☐ Delivered

Order Form

ORDER NO:

DATE:

ORDER NAME:

✓

Customer Details

Name :

Company:

Phone:

Email :

Address:

Order Details

#	Item/Description	Qty	Price	Discount	Total
☐					
☐					
☐					
☐					
☐					
☐					
☐					
☐					
☐					
☐					

TOTAL

Payment Details

Subtotal :

Delivery :

Discount:

TAX   :

Date

Total

Status

☐ Paid   ☐ Half Paid   ☐ Pending

Payment Method

☐ Cash   ☐ Credit Card   ☐ Bank   ☐ PayPal

☐ Other :

Delivery Details

Delivery Date :

Method   :   ☐ Pick-up   ☐ Delivery

Tracking No

Status

☐ Started   ☐ Finished   ☐ Delivered

Special Notes

Order Form - Small Orders

Name :

Address:

Phone: **Email :**

ORDER NO:

DATE:

ORDER NAME: ✓

Order Details

#	Item/Description	Qty	Price	Discount	Total
☐					
☐					
☐					
☐					
☐					

Notes: **TOTAL**

Payment Details

Subtotal :

Delivery :

Discount: **TAX:**

Method :

Date

Total

Status
☐ Paid ☐ Half Paid ☐ Pending

Delivery Details

Delivery Date :

Method : ☐ Pick-up ☐ Delivery

Tracking No

Status
☐ Started ☐ Finished ☐ Delivered

Order Form - Small Orders

Name :

Address:

Phone: **Email :**

ORDER NO:

DATE:

ORDER NAME: ✓

Order Details

#	Item/Description	Qty	Price	Discount	Total
☐					
☐					
☐					
☐					
☐					

Notes: **TOTAL**

Payment Details

Subtotal :

Delivery :

Discount: **TAX:**

Method :

Date

Total

Status
☐ Paid ☐ Half Paid ☐ Pending

Delivery Details

Delivery Date :

Method : ☐ Pick-up ☐ Delivery

Tracking No

Status
☐ Started ☐ Finished ☐ Delivered

Order Form

ORDER NO:

DATE:

ORDER NAME:

✓

Customer Details

Name :

Company:

Phone: Email :

Address:

Order Details

#	Item/Description	Qty	Price	Discount	Total
☐					
☐					
☐					
☐					
☐					
☐					
☐					
☐					
☐					
☐					
				TOTAL	

Payment Details

Subtotal :

Delivery :

Discount:

TAX   :

Date

Total

Status

☐ Paid   ☐ Half Paid   ☐ Pending

Payment Method

☐ Cash ☐ Credit Card ☐ Bank ☐ PayPal

☐ Other :

Special Notes

Delivery Details

Delivery Date :

Method   : ☐ Pick-up ☐ Delivery

Tracking No

Status

☐ Started   ☐ Finished   ☐ Delivered

Order Form

ORDER NO: _____   DATE: _____

ORDER NAME: _____   ✓ ☐

Customer Details

Name : _____   Address: _____

Company: _____   _____

Phone: _____   Email : _____   _____

Order Details

☐	#	Item/Description	Qty	Price	Discount	Total
☐						
☐						
☐						
☐						
☐						
☐						
☐						
☐						
☐						
☐						

TOTAL _____

Payment Details

Subtotal : _____

Delivery : _____

Discount : _____

TAX : _____

Date _____

Total _____

Status
☐ Paid   ☐ Half Paid   ☐ Pending

Payment Method
☐ Cash   ☐ Credit Card   ☐ Bank   ☐ PayPal
☐ Other : _____

Delivery Details

Delivery Date : _____

Method : ☐ Pick-up   ☐ Delivery

Tracking No _____

Status
☐ Started   ☐ Finished   ☐ Delivered

Special Notes

Order Form

ORDER NO:

DATE:

ORDER NAME:

✓

Customer Details

Name :

Company:

Phone:

Email :

Address:

Order Details

	#	Item/Description	Qty	Price	Discount	Total
☐						
☐						
☐						
☐						
☐						
☐						
☐						
☐						
☐						
☐						

TOTAL

Payment Details

Subtotal :

Delivery :

Discount :

TAX :

Date

Total

Status
☐ Paid ☐ Half Paid ☐ Pending

Payment Method
☐ Cash ☐ Credit Card ☐ Bank ☐ PayPal
☐ Other :

Special Notes

Delivery Details

Delivery Date :

Method : ☐ Pick-up ☐ Delivery

Tracking No

Status
☐ Started ☐ Finished ☐ Delivered

Order Form - Small Orders

Name :

Address:

Phone: **Email :**

ORDER NO:

DATE:

ORDER NAME: ✓

Order Details

#	Item/Description	Qty	Price	Discount	Total
☐					
☐					
☐					
☐					
☐					

Notes: **TOTAL**

Payment Details

Subtotal :

Delivery :

Discount: **TAX:**

Method :

Date

Total

Status
☐ Paid ☐ Half Paid ☐ Pending

Delivery Details

Delivery Date :

Method   : ☐ Pick-up   ☐ Delivery

Tracking No

Status
☐ Started ☐ Finished ☐ Delivered

Order Form - Small Orders

Name :

Address:

Phone: **Email :**

ORDER NO:

DATE:

ORDER NAME: ✓

Order Details

#	Item/Description	Qty	Price	Discount	Total
☐					
☐					
☐					
☐					
☐					

Notes: **TOTAL**

Payment Details

Subtotal :

Delivery :

Discount: **TAX:**

Method :

Date

Total

Status
☐ Paid ☐ Half Paid ☐ Pending

Delivery Details

Delivery Date :

Method   : ☐ Pick-up   ☐ Delivery

Tracking No

Status
☐ Started ☐ Finished ☐ Delivered

Order Form

ORDER NO:

DATE:

ORDER NAME:

✓

Customer Details

Name :

Address:

Company:

Phone:

Email :

Order Details

	#	Item/Description	Qty	Price	Discount	Total
☐						
☐						
☐						
☐						
☐						
☐						
☐						
☐						
☐						
☐						

TOTAL

Payment Details

Subtotal :

Delivery :

Discount :

TAX :

Date

Total

Status

☐ Paid ☐ Half Paid ☐ Pending

Payment Method

☐ Cash ☐ Credit Card ☐ Bank ☐ PayPal

☐ Other :

Special Notes

Delivery Details

Delivery Date :

Method : ☐ Pick-up ☐ Delivery

Tracking No

Status

☐ Started ☐ Finished ☐ Delivered

Order Form

ORDER NO:

DATE:

ORDER NAME:

✓

Customer Details

Name :

Address:

Company:

Phone:

Email :

Order Details

#	Item/Description	Qty	Price	Discount	Total
☐					
☐					
☐					
☐					
☐					
☐					
☐					
☐					
☐					
☐					

TOTAL

Payment Details

Subtotal :

Delivery :

Discount :

TAX :

Date

Total

Status

☐ Paid   ☐ Half Paid   ☐ Pending

Payment Method

☐ Cash   ☐ Credit Card   ☐ Bank   ☐ PayPal

☐ Other :

Delivery Details

Delivery Date :

Method : ☐ Pick-up   ☐ Delivery

Tracking No

Status

☐ Started   ☐ Finished   ☐ Delivered

Special Notes

Order Form

ORDER NO:

DATE:

ORDER NAME:

✓

Customer Details

Name : _____

Address: _____

Company: _____

_____

Phone: _____   Email : _____

Order Details

	#	Item/Description	Qty	Price	Discount	Total
☐						
☐						
☐						
☐						
☐						
☐						
☐						
☐						
☐						
☐						

TOTAL

Payment Details

Subtotal : _____

Delivery : _____

Discount: _____

TAX   : _____

Date

Total

Status

☐ Paid ☐ Half Paid ☐ Pending

Payment Method

☐ Cash ☐ Credit Card ☐ Bank ☐ PayPal

☐ Other :

Delivery Details

Delivery Date : _____

Method   : ☐ Pick-up   ☐ Delivery

Tracking No

Status

☐ Started ☐ Finished ☐ Delivered

Special Notes

Order Form - Small Orders

Name : _____

Address: _____

Phone: _____ **Email :** _____

ORDER NO: _____

DATE: _____

ORDER NAME: _____ ✓

Order Details

	#	Item/Description	Qty	Price	Discount	Total
☐						
☐						
☐						
☐						
☐						

Notes: **TOTAL** _____

Payment Details

Subtotal : _____

Delivery : _____

Discount: _____ **TAX:** _____

Method : _____

Date _____

Total _____

Status
☐ Paid ☐ Half Paid ☐ Pending

Delivery Details

Delivery Date : _____

Method : ☐ Pick-up ☐ Delivery

Tracking No _____

Status
☐ Started ☐ Finished ☐ Delivered

Order Form - Small Orders

Name : _____

Address: _____

Phone: _____ **Email :** _____

ORDER NO: _____

DATE: _____

ORDER NAME: _____ ✓

Order Details

	#	Item/Description	Qty	Price	Discount	Total
☐						
☐						
☐						
☐						
☐						

Notes: **TOTAL** _____

Payment Details

Subtotal : _____

Delivery : _____

Discount: _____ **TAX:** _____

Method : _____

Date _____

Total _____

Status
☐ Paid ☐ Half Paid ☐ Pending

Delivery Details

Delivery Date : _____

Method : ☐ Pick-up ☐ Delivery

Tracking No _____

Status
☐ Started ☐ Finished ☐ Delivered

Order Form

ORDER NO:

DATE:

ORDER NAME:

✓

Customer Details

Name :

Company:

Phone:

Email :

Address:

Order Details

	#	Item/Description	Qty	Price	Discount	Total
☐						
☐						
☐						
☐						
☐						
☐						
☐						
☐						
☐						
☐						

TOTAL

Payment Details

Subtotal :

Delivery :

Discount :

TAX :

Date

Total

Status

☐ Paid   ☐ Half Paid   ☐ Pending

Payment Method

☐ Cash ☐ Credit Card ☐ Bank ☐ PayPal
☐ Other :

Delivery Details

Delivery Date :

Method : ☐ Pick-up ☐ Delivery

Tracking No

Status

☐ Started   ☐ Finished   ☐ Delivered

Special Notes

Order Form

ORDER NO:

DATE:

ORDER NAME:

✓

Customer Details

Name :

Company:

Phone:

Email :

Address:

Order Details

	#	Item/Description	Qty	Price	Discount	Total
☐						
☐						
☐						
☐						
☐						
☐						
☐						
☐						
☐						
☐						
					TOTAL	

Payment Details

Subtotal :

Delivery :

Discount :

TAX :

Date

Total

Status

☐ Paid   ☐ Half Paid   ☐ Pending

Payment Method

☐ Cash   ☐ Credit Card   ☐ Bank   ☐ PayPal

☐ Other :

Delivery Details

Delivery Date :

Method : ☐ Pick-up ☐ Delivery

Tracking No

Status

☐ Started   ☐ Finished   ☐ Delivered

Special Notes

Order Form

ORDER NO:

DATE:

ORDER NAME:

✓

Customer Details

Name :

Company:

Phone:

Email :

Address:

Order Details

	#	Item/Description	Qty	Price	Discount	Total
☐						
☐						
☐						
☐						
☐						
☐						
☐						
☐						
☐						
☐						

TOTAL

Payment Details

Subtotal :

Delivery :

Discount:

TAX :

Date

Total

Status

☐ Paid   ☐ Half Paid   ☐ Pending

Payment Method

☐ Cash   ☐ Credit Card   ☐ Bank   ☐ PayPal

☐ Other :

Special Notes

Delivery Details

Delivery Date :

Method : ☐ Pick-up   ☐ Delivery

Tracking No

Status

☐ Started   ☐ Finished   ☐ Delivered

Order Form - Small Orders

Name : _____

Address: _____

Phone: _____ **Email :** _____

ORDER NO: _____

DATE: _____

ORDER NAME: _____

✓

Order Details

	#	Item/Description	Qty	Price	Discount	Total
☐						
☐						
☐						
☐						
☐						

Notes:

TOTAL

Payment Details

Subtotal : _____

Delivery : _____

Discount: _____ **TAX:** _____

Method : _____

Date

Total

Status
☐ Paid ☐ Half Paid ☐ Pending

Delivery Details

Delivery Date : _____

Method : ☐ Pick-up ☐ Delivery

Tracking No

Status
☐ Started ☐ Finished ☐ Delivered

Order Form - Small Orders

Name : _____

Address: _____

Phone: _____ **Email :** _____

ORDER NO: _____

DATE: _____

ORDER NAME: _____

✓

Order Details

	#	Item/Description	Qty	Price	Discount	Total
☐						
☐						
☐						
☐						
☐						

Notes:

TOTAL

Payment Details

Subtotal : _____

Delivery : _____

Discount: _____ **TAX:** _____

Method : _____

Date

Total

Status
☐ Paid ☐ Half Paid ☐ Pending

Delivery Details

Delivery Date : _____

Method : ☐ Pick-up ☐ Delivery

Tracking No

Status
☐ Started ☐ Finished ☐ Delivered

Order Form

ORDER NO:

DATE:

ORDER NAME:

✓

Customer Details

Name :

Address:

Company:

Phone:

Email :

Order Details

#	Item/Description	Qty	Price	Discount	Total
☐					
☐					
☐					
☐					
☐					
☐					
☐					
☐					
☐					
☐					

TOTAL

Payment Details

Subtotal :

Delivery :

Discount:

TAX   :

Date

Total

Status

☐ Paid   ☐ Half Paid   ☐ Pending

Payment Method

☐ Cash   ☐ Credit Card   ☐ Bank   ☐ PayPal

☐ Other :

Special Notes

Delivery Details

Delivery Date :

Method   :   ☐ Pick-up   ☐ Delivery

Tracking No

Status

☐ Started   ☐ Finished   ☐ Delivered

Order Form

ORDER NO:

DATE:

ORDER NAME:

✓

Customer Details

Name :

Address:

Company:

Phone:

Email :

Order Details

#	Item/Description	Qty	Price	Discount	Total
☐					
☐					
☐					
☐					
☐					
☐					
☐					
☐					
☐					
☐					

TOTAL

Payment Details

Subtotal :

Delivery :

Discount :

TAX :

Payment Method

☐ Cash ☐ Credit Card ☐ Bank ☐ PayPal

☐ Other :

Date

Total

Status

☐ Paid ☐ Half Paid ☐ Pending

Special Notes

Delivery Details

Delivery Date :

Method : ☐ Pick-up ☐ Delivery

Tracking No

Status

☐ Started ☐ Finished ☐ Delivered

Order Form

ORDER NO:

DATE:

ORDER NAME:

✓

Customer Details

Name :

Address:

Company:

Phone:

Email :

Order Details

	#	Item/Description	Qty	Price	Discount	Total
☐						
☐						
☐						
☐						
☐						
☐						
☐						
☐						
☐						
☐						

TOTAL

Payment Details

Subtotal :

Delivery :

Discount :

TAX :

Date

Total

Status

☐ Paid ☐ Half Paid ☐ Pending

Payment Method

☐ Cash ☐ Credit Card ☐ Bank ☐ PayPal

☐ Other :

Delivery Details

Delivery Date :

Method : ☐ Pick-up ☐ Delivery

Tracking No

Status

☐ Started ☐ Finished ☐ Delivered

Special Notes

Order Form - Small Orders

Name : _____

Address: _____

Phone: _____ **Email :** _____

ORDER NO: _____

DATE: _____

ORDER NAME: _____ ✓

Order Details

#	Item/Description	Qty	Price	Discount	Total
☐					
☐					
☐					
☐					
☐					

Notes: **TOTAL** _____

Payment Details

Subtotal : _____

Delivery : _____

Discount: _____ **TAX:** _____

Method : _____

Date _____

Total _____

Status
☐ Paid ☐ Half Paid ☐ Pending

Delivery Details

Delivery Date : _____

Method : ☐ Pick-up ☐ Delivery

Tracking No _____

Status
☐ Started ☐ Finished ☐ Delivered

Order Form - Small Orders

Name : _____

Address: _____

Phone: _____ **Email :** _____

ORDER NO: _____

DATE: _____

ORDER NAME: _____ ✓

Order Details

#	Item/Description	Qty	Price	Discount	Total
☐					
☐					
☐					
☐					
☐					

Notes: **TOTAL** _____

Payment Details

Subtotal : _____

Delivery : _____

Discount: _____ **TAX:** _____

Method : _____

Date _____

Total _____

Status
☐ Paid ☐ Half Paid ☐ Pending

Delivery Details

Delivery Date : _____

Method : ☐ Pick-up ☐ Delivery

Tracking No _____

Status
☐ Started ☐ Finished ☐ Delivered

Order Form

ORDER NO:

DATE:

ORDER NAME:

✓

Customer Details

Name :

Address:

Company:

Phone:

Email :

Order Details

	#	Item/Description	Qty	Price	Discount	Total
☐						
☐						
☐						
☐						
☐						
☐						
☐						
☐						
☐						
☐						

TOTAL

Payment Details

Date

Subtotal :

Total

Delivery :

Discount:

Status

TAX :

☐ Paid ☐ Half Paid ☐ Pending

Payment Method

☐ Cash ☐ Credit Card ☐ Bank ☐ PayPal

☐ Other :

Special Notes

Delivery Details

Delivery Date :

Method : ☐ Pick-up ☐ Delivery

Tracking No

Status

☐ Started ☐ Finished ☐ Delivered

Order Form

ORDER NO:

DATE:

ORDER NAME:

✓

Customer Details

Name :

Address:

Company:

Phone:

Email :

Order Details

#	Item/Description	Qty	Price	Discount	Total
☐					
☐					
☐					
☐					
☐					
☐					
☐					
☐					
☐					
☐					

TOTAL

Payment Details

Subtotal :

Delivery :

Discount :

TAX :

Date

Total

Status
☐ Paid   ☐ Half Paid   ☐ Pending

Payment Method
☐ Cash   ☐ Credit Card   ☐ Bank   ☐ PayPal
☐ Other :

Delivery Details

Delivery Date :

Method : ☐ Pick-up   ☐ Delivery

Tracking No

Status
☐ Started   ☐ Finished   ☐ Delivered

Special Notes

Order Form

ORDER NO:

DATE:

ORDER NAME:

✓

Customer Details

Name :

Company:

Phone:

Email :

Address:

Order Details

	#	Item/Description	Qty	Price	Discount	Total
☐						
☐						
☐						
☐						
☐						
☐						
☐						
☐						
☐						
☐						

TOTAL

Payment Details

Subtotal :

Delivery :

Discount :

TAX :

Date

Total

Status

☐ Paid ☐ Half Paid ☐ Pending

Payment Method

☐ Cash ☐ Credit Card ☐ Bank ☐ PayPal

☐ Other :

Delivery Details

Delivery Date :

Method : ☐ Pick-up ☐ Delivery

Tracking No

Status

☐ Started ☐ Finished ☐ Delivered

Special Notes

Order Form - Small Orders

Name :

Address:

Phone: Email :

ORDER NO:

DATE:

ORDER NAME: ✓

Order Details

#	Item/Description	Qty	Price	Discount	Total
☐					
☐					
☐					
☐					
☐					

Notes: **TOTAL**

Payment Details

Subtotal :

Delivery :

Discount: TAX:

Method   :

Date

Total

Status
☐ Paid   ☐ Half Paid   ☐ Pending

Delivery Details

Delivery Date :

Method   :   ☐ Pick-up   ☐ Delivery

Tracking No   Status
☐ Started ☐ Finished ☐ Delivered

Order Form - Small Orders

Name :

Address:

Phone: Email :

ORDER NO:

DATE:

ORDER NAME: ✓

Order Details

#	Item/Description	Qty	Price	Discount	Total
☐					
☐					
☐					
☐					
☐					

Notes: **TOTAL**

Payment Details

Subtotal :

Delivery :

Discount: TAX:

Method   :

Date

Total

Status
☐ Paid   ☐ Half Paid   ☐ Pending

Delivery Details

Delivery Date :

Method   :   ☐ Pick-up   ☐ Delivery

Tracking No   Status
☐ Started ☐ Finished ☐ Delivered

Order Form

ORDER NO:

DATE:

ORDER NAME:

✓

Customer Details

Name :

Company:

Phone: Email :

Address:

Order Details

	#	Item/Description	Qty	Price	Discount	Total
☐						
☐						
☐						
☐						
☐						
☐						
☐						
☐						
☐						
☐						

TOTAL

Payment Details

Subtotal :

Delivery :

Discount :

TAX   :

Date

Total

Status

☐ Paid   ☐ Half Paid   ☐ Pending

Payment Method

☐ Cash ☐ Credit Card ☐ Bank ☐ PayPal

☐ Other :

Delivery Details

Delivery Date :

Method   : ☐ Pick-up   ☐ Delivery

Tracking No

Status

☐ Started   ☐ Finished   ☐ Delivered

Special Notes

Order Form

ORDER NO: _____ DATE: _____

ORDER NAME: _____ ✓

Customer Details

Name : _____ Address: _____

Company: _____ _____

Phone: _____ Email : _____ _____

Order Details

☐	#	Item/Description	Qty	Price	Discount	Total
☐						
☐						
☐						
☐						
☐						
☐						
☐						
☐						
☐						
☐						

TOTAL _____

Payment Details

Subtotal : _____

Delivery : _____

Discount : _____

TAX : _____

Date _____

Total _____

Status

☐ Paid ☐ Half Paid ☐ Pending

Payment Method

☐ Cash ☐ Credit Card ☐ Bank ☐ PayPal

☐ Other : _____

Delivery Details

Delivery Date : _____

Method : ☐ Pick-up ☐ Delivery

Tracking No _____

Status

☐ Started ☐ Finished ☐ Delivered

Special Notes

Order Form

ORDER NO: _____

DATE: _____

ORDER NAME: _____ ✓ ☐

Customer Details

Name : _____

Company: _____

Phone: _____   Email : _____

Address: _____

Order Details

#	Item/Description	Qty	Price	Discount	Total
☐					
☐					
☐					
☐					
☐					
☐					
☐					
☐					
☐					
☐					

TOTAL _____

Payment Details

Subtotal : _____

Delivery : _____

Discount : _____

TAX : _____

Date _____

Total _____

Status
☐ Paid   ☐ Half Paid   ☐ Pending

Payment Method
☐ Cash ☐ Credit Card ☐ Bank ☐ PayPal
☐ Other : _____

Delivery Details

Delivery Date : _____

Method : ☐ Pick-up ☐ Delivery

Tracking No _____

Status
☐ Started   ☐ Finished   ☐ Delivered

Special Notes

Order Form - Small Orders

Name :

Address:

Phone: **Email :**

ORDER NAME: ✓

Order Details

#	Item/Description	Qty	Price	Discount	Total
☐					
☐					
☐					
☐					
☐					

Notes: **TOTAL**

Payment Details

Subtotal :

Delivery :

Discount: **TAX:**

Method :

Date

Total

Status
☐ Paid   ☐ Half Paid   ☐ Pending

Delivery Details

Delivery Date :

Method   :   ☐ Pick-up   ☐ Delivery

Tracking No

Status
☐ Started   ☐ Finished   ☐ Delivered

Order Form - Small Orders

Name :

Address:

Phone: **Email :**

ORDER NO: **DATE:**

ORDER NAME: ✓

Order Details

#	Item/Description	Qty	Price	Discount	Total
☐					
☐					
☐					
☐					
☐					

Notes: **TOTAL**

Payment Details

Subtotal :

Delivery :

Discount: **TAX:**

Method :

Date

Total

Status
☐ Paid   ☐ Half Paid   ☐ Pending

Delivery Details

Delivery Date :

Method   :   ☐ Pick-up   ☐ Delivery

Tracking No

Status
☐ Started   ☐ Finished   ☐ Delivered

Order Form

ORDER NO:

DATE:

ORDER NAME:

✓

Customer Details

Name :

Company:

Phone:

Email :

Address:

Order Details

☐ #	Item/Description	Qty	Price	Discount	Total
☐					
☐					
☐					
☐					
☐					
☐					
☐					
☐					
☐					
☐					
				TOTAL	

Payment Details

Subtotal :

Delivery :

Discount :

TAX :

Date

Total

Status
☐ Paid   ☐ Half Paid   ☐ Pending

Payment Method
☐ Cash   ☐ Credit Card   ☐ Bank   ☐ PayPal
☐ Other :

Delivery Details

Delivery Date :

Method : ☐ Pick-up ☐ Delivery

Tracking No

Status
☐ Started   ☐ Finished   ☐ Delivered

Special Notes

Order Form

ORDER NO:

DATE:

ORDER NAME:

✓

Customer Details

Name :

Address:

Company:

Phone:

Email :

Order Details

	#	Item/Description	Qty	Price	Discount	Total
☐						
☐						
☐						
☐						
☐						
☐						
☐						
☐						
☐						
☐						
☐						

TOTAL

Payment Details

Subtotal :

Delivery :

Discount :

TAX :

Date

Total

Status

☐ Paid   ☐ Half Paid   ☐ Pending

Payment Method

☐ Cash   ☐ Credit Card   ☐ Bank   ☐ PayPal

☐ Other :

Special Notes

Delivery Details

Delivery Date :

Method   :   ☐ Pick-up   ☐ Delivery

Tracking No

Status

☐ Started   ☐ Finished   ☐ Delivered

Order Form

ORDER NO:

DATE:

ORDER NAME:

✓

Customer Details

Name :

Company:

Phone:

Email :

Address:

Order Details

	#	Item/Description	Qty	Price	Discount	Total
☐						
☐						
☐						
☐						
☐						
☐						
☐						
☐						
☐						
☐						
					TOTAL	

Payment Details

Subtotal :

Delivery :

Discount :

TAX :

Date

Total

Status
☐ Paid ☐ Half Paid ☐ Pending

Payment Method
☐ Cash ☐ Credit Card ☐ Bank ☐ PayPal
☐ Other :

Special Notes

Delivery Details

Delivery Date :

Method : ☐ Pick-up ☐ Delivery

Tracking No

Status
☐ Started ☐ Finished ☐ Delivered

Order Form - Small Orders

Name :

Address:

Phone: **Email :**

ORDER NO:

DATE:

ORDER NAME: ✓

Order Details

#	Item/Description	Qty	Price	Discount	Total
☐					
☐					
☐					
☐					
☐					

Notes: **TOTAL**

Payment Details

Subtotal :

Delivery :

Discount: **TAX:**

Method :

Date

Total

Status
☐ Paid   ☐ Half Paid   ☐ Pending

Delivery Details

Delivery Date :

Method   : ☐ Pick-up   ☐ Delivery

Tracking No

Status
☐ Started   ☐ Finished   ☐ Delivered

Order Form - Small Orders

Name :

Address:

Phone: **Email :**

ORDER NO:

DATE:

ORDER NAME: ✓

Order Details

#	Item/Description	Qty	Price	Discount	Total
☐					
☐					
☐					
☐					
☐					

Notes: **TOTAL**

Payment Details

Subtotal :

Delivery :

Discount: **TAX:**

Method :

Date

Total

Status
☐ Paid   ☐ Half Paid   ☐ Pending

Delivery Details

Delivery Date :

Method   : ☐ Pick-up   ☐ Delivery

Tracking No

Status
☐ Started   ☐ Finished   ☐ Delivered

Order Form

ORDER NO:

DATE:

ORDER NAME:

✓

Customer Details

Name :

Address:

Company:

Phone:

Email :

Order Details

	#	Item/Description	Qty	Price	Discount	Total
☐						
☐						
☐						
☐						
☐						
☐						
☐						
☐						
☐						
☐						

TOTAL

Payment Details

Subtotal :

Delivery :

Discount :

TAX :

Date

Total

Status
☐ Paid ☐ Half Paid ☐ Pending

Payment Method
☐ Cash ☐ Credit Card ☐ Bank ☐ PayPal
☐ Other :

Delivery Details

Delivery Date :

Method : ☐ Pick-up ☐ Delivery

Tracking No

Status
☐ Started ☐ Finished ☐ Delivered

Special Notes

Order Form

ORDER NO:

DATE:

ORDER NAME:

✓

Customer Details

Name :

Address:

Company:

Phone: Email :

Order Details

	#	Item/Description	Qty	Price	Discount	Total
☐						
☐						
☐						
☐						
☐						
☐						
☐						
☐						
☐						
☐						
					TOTAL	

Payment Details

Subtotal :

Delivery :

Discount:

TAX   :

Date

Total

Status

☐ Paid   ☐ Half Paid   ☐ Pending

Payment Method

☐ Cash ☐ Credit Card ☐ Bank ☐ PayPal

☐ Other :

Special Notes

Delivery Details

Delivery Date :

Method   : ☐ Pick-up ☐ Delivery

Tracking No

Status

☐ Started   ☐ Finished   ☐ Delivered

Order Form

ORDER NO:

DATE:

ORDER NAME:

✓

Customer Details

Name :

Address:

Company:

Phone:

Email :

Order Details

	#	Item/Description	Qty	Price	Discount	Total
☐						
☐						
☐						
☐						
☐						
☐						
☐						
☐						
☐						
☐						

TOTAL

Payment Details

Subtotal :

Delivery :

Discount :

TAX :

Date

Total

Status

☐ Paid ☐ Half Paid ☐ Pending

Payment Method

☐ Cash ☐ Credit Card ☐ Bank ☐ PayPal

☐ Other :

Delivery Details

Delivery Date :

Method : ☐ Pick-up ☐ Delivery

Tracking No

Status

☐ Started ☐ Finished ☐ Delivered

Special Notes

Order Form - Small Orders

Name :

Address:

Phone: **Email :**

ORDER NO:

DATE:

ORDER NAME: ✓

Order Details

#	Item/Description	Qty	Price	Discount	Total
☐					
☐					
☐					
☐					
☐					

Notes: **TOTAL**

Payment Details

Subtotal :

Delivery :

Discount: **TAX:**

Method :

Date

Total

Status
☐ Paid   ☐ Half Paid   ☐ Pending

Delivery Details

Delivery Date :

Method :   ☐ Pick-up   ☐ Delivery

Tracking No

Status
☐ Started   ☐ Finished   ☐ Delivered

Order Form - Small Orders

Name :

Address:

Phone: **Email :**

ORDER NO:

DATE:

ORDER NAME: ✓

Order Details

#	Item/Description	Qty	Price	Discount	Total
☐					
☐					
☐					
☐					
☐					

Notes: **TOTAL**

Payment Details

Subtotal :

Delivery :

Discount: **TAX:**

Method :

Date

Total

Status
☐ Paid   ☐ Half Paid   ☐ Pending

Delivery Details

Delivery Date :

Method :   ☐ Pick-up   ☐ Delivery

Tracking No

Status
☐ Started   ☐ Finished   ☐ Delivered

Order Form

ORDER NO: _____

DATE: _____

ORDER NAME: _____ ✓ ☐

Customer Details

Name : _____

Company: _____

Phone: _____   Email : _____

Address: _____

_____

_____

Order Details

☐	#	Item/Description	Qty	Price	Discount	Total
☐						
☐						
☐						
☐						
☐						
☐						
☐						
☐						
☐						
☐						
					TOTAL	

Payment Details

Subtotal : _____

Delivery : _____

Discount: _____

TAX : _____

Date _____

Total _____

Status
☐ Paid   ☐ Half Paid   ☐ Pending

Payment Method
☐ Cash   ☐ Credit Card   ☐ Bank   ☐ PayPal
☐ Other : _____

Delivery Details

Delivery Date : _____

Method : ☐ Pick-up   ☐ Delivery

Tracking No _____

Status
☐ Started   ☐ Finished   ☐ Delivered

Special Notes

Order Form

ORDER NO: _____ DATE: _____

ORDER NAME: _____ ✓ ☐

Customer Details

Name : _____ Address: _____

Company: _____ _____

Phone: _____ Email : _____

Order Details

	#	Item/Description	Qty	Price	Discount	Total
☐						
☐						
☐						
☐						
☐						
☐						
☐						
☐						
☐						
☐						

TOTAL _____

Payment Details

Subtotal : _____

Delivery : _____

Discount : _____

TAX : _____

Date
_____

Total
_____

Status
☐ Paid   ☐ Half Paid   ☐ Pending

Payment Method

☐ Cash   ☐ Credit Card   ☐ Bank   ☐ PayPal

☐ Other : _____

Delivery Details

Delivery Date : _____

Method : ☐ Pick-up   ☐ Delivery

Tracking No
_____

Status
☐ Started   ☐ Finished   ☐ Delivered

Special Notes

Order Form

ORDER NO:

DATE:

ORDER NAME:

✓

Customer Details

Name :

Address:

Company:

Phone:

Email :

Order Details

	#	Item/Description	Qty	Price	Discount	Total
☐						
☐						
☐						
☐						
☐						
☐						
☐						
☐						
☐						
☐						

TOTAL

Payment Details

Subtotal :

Delivery :

Discount :

TAX :

Date

Total

Status
☐ Paid ☐ Half Paid ☐ Pending

Payment Method
☐ Cash ☐ Credit Card ☐ Bank ☐ PayPal
☐ Other :

Special Notes

Delivery Details

Delivery Date :

Method : ☐ Pick-up ☐ Delivery

Tracking No

Status
☐ Started ☐ Finished ☐ Delivered

Order Form - Small Orders

Name :

Address:

Phone: **Email :**

ORDER NO:

DATE:

ORDER NAME: ✓

Order Details

#	Item/Description	Qty	Price	Discount	Total
☐					
☐					
☐					
☐					
☐					

Notes: **TOTAL**

Payment Details

Subtotal :

Delivery :

Discount: **TAX:**

Method :

Date

Total

Status
☐ Paid   ☐ Half Paid   ☐ Pending

Delivery Details

Delivery Date :

Method :   ☐ Pick-up   ☐ Delivery

Tracking No

Status
☐ Started   ☐ Finished   ☐ Delivered

Order Form - Small Orders

Name :

Address:

Phone: **Email :**

ORDER NO:

DATE:

ORDER NAME: ✓

Order Details

#	Item/Description	Qty	Price	Discount	Total
☐					
☐					
☐					
☐					
☐					

Notes: **TOTAL**

Payment Details

Subtotal :

Delivery :

Discount: **TAX:**

Method :

Date

Total

Status
☐ Paid   ☐ Half Paid   ☐ Pending

Delivery Details

Delivery Date :

Method :   ☐ Pick-up   ☐ Delivery

Tracking No

Status
☐ Started   ☐ Finished   ☐ Delivered

Order Form

ORDER NO:

DATE:

ORDER NAME:

✓

Customer Details

Name :

Address:

Company:

Phone:

Email :

Order Details

	#	Item/Description	Qty	Price	Discount	Total
☐						
☐						
☐						
☐						
☐						
☐						
☐						
☐						
☐						
☐						

TOTAL

Payment Details

Subtotal :

Delivery :

Discount:

TAX :

Date

Total

Status
☐ Paid ☐ Half Paid ☐ Pending

Payment Method
☐ Cash ☐ Credit Card ☐ Bank ☐ PayPal
☐ Other :

Delivery Details

Delivery Date :

Method : ☐ Pick-up ☐ Delivery

Tracking No

Status
☐ Started ☐ Finished ☐ Delivered

Special Notes

Order Form

ORDER NO:

DATE:

ORDER NAME:

✓

Customer Details

Name :

Company:

Phone:

Email :

Address:

Order Details

#	Item/Description	Qty	Price	Discount	Total
☐					
☐					
☐					
☐					
☐					
☐					
☐					
☐					
☐					
☐					

TOTAL

Payment Details

Subtotal :

Delivery :

Discount :

TAX :

Date

Total

Status

☐ Paid   ☐ Half Paid   ☐ Pending

Payment Method

☐ Cash   ☐ Credit Card   ☐ Bank   ☐ PayPal

☐ Other :

Delivery Details

Delivery Date :

Method : ☐ Pick-up   ☐ Delivery

Tracking No

Status

☐ Started   ☐ Finished   ☐ Delivered

Special Notes

Order Form

ORDER NO:

DATE:

ORDER NAME:

✓

Customer Details

Name :

Company:

Phone: Email :

Address:

Order Details

	#	Item/Description	Qty	Price	Discount	Total
☐						
☐						
☐						
☐						
☐						
☐						
☐						
☐						
☐						
☐						

TOTAL

Payment Details

Subtotal :

Delivery :

Discount:

TAX   :

Date

Total

Status
☐ Paid   ☐ Half Paid   ☐ Pending

Payment Method
☐ Cash   ☐ Credit Card   ☐ Bank   ☐ PayPal
☐ Other :

Special Notes

Delivery Details

Delivery Date :

Method   :   ☐ Pick-up   ☐ Delivery

Tracking No

Status
☐ Started   ☐ Finished   ☐ Delivered

Order Form - Small Orders

Name :

Address:

Phone:　　　　　**Email :**

ORDER NO:

DATE:

ORDER NAME:　　　　　　　　　　　　✓

Order Details

	#	Item/Description	Qty	Price	Discount	Total
☐						
☐						
☐						
☐						
☐						

Notes:　　　　　　　　　　　　　　　　**TOTAL**

Payment Details

Subtotal :

Delivery :

Discount:　　　**TAX:**

Method :

Date

Total

Status
☐ Paid　☐ Half Paid　☐ Pending

Delivery Details

Delivery Date :

Method : ☐ Pick-up　☐ Delivery

Tracking No

Status
☐ Started　☐ Finished　☐ Delivered

Order Form - Small Orders

Name :

Address:

Phone:　　　　　**Email :**

ORDER NO:

DATE:

ORDER NAME:　　　　　　　　　　　　✓

Order Details

	#	Item/Description	Qty	Price	Discount	Total
☐						
☐						
☐						
☐						
☐						

Notes:　　　　　　　　　　　　　　　　**TOTAL**

Payment Details

Subtotal :

Delivery :

Discount:　　　**TAX:**

Method :

Date

Total

Status
☐ Paid　☐ Half Paid　☐ Pending

Delivery Details

Delivery Date :

Method : ☐ Pick-up　☐ Delivery

Tracking No

Status
☐ Started　☐ Finished　☐ Delivered

Order Form

ORDER NO:

DATE:

ORDER NAME:

✓

Customer Details

Name :

Company:

Phone:

Email :

Address:

Order Details

	#	Item/Description	Qty	Price	Discount	Total
☐						
☐						
☐						
☐						
☐						
☐						
☐						
☐						
☐						
☐						

TOTAL

Payment Details

Subtotal :

Delivery :

Discount :

TAX :

Date

Total

Status

☐ Paid ☐ Half Paid ☐ Pending

┌ Payment Method ┐

☐ Cash ☐ Credit Card ☐ Bank ☐ PayPal

☐ Other :

Special Notes

Delivery Details

Delivery Date :

Method : ☐ Pick-up ☐ Delivery

┌ Tracking No ┐   ┌ Status ┐

☐ Started ☐ Finished ☐ Delivered

Order Form

ORDER NO:

DATE:

ORDER NAME:

✓

Customer Details

Name :

Company:

Phone:

Email :

Address:

Order Details

#	Item/Description	Qty	Price	Discount	Total
☐					
☐					
☐					
☐					
☐					
☐					
☐					
☐					
☐					
☐					

TOTAL

Payment Details

Subtotal :

Delivery :

Discount :

TAX :

Date

Total

Status

☐ Paid   ☐ Half Paid   ☐ Pending

Payment Method

☐ Cash   ☐ Credit Card   ☐ Bank   ☐ PayPal

☐ Other :

Delivery Details

Delivery Date :

Method   :   ☐ Pick-up   ☐ Delivery

Tracking No

Status

☐ Started   ☐ Finished   ☐ Delivered

Special Notes

Order Form

ORDER NO:

DATE:

ORDER NAME:

✓

Customer Details

Name :

Address:

Company:

Phone:

Email :

Order Details

	#	Item/Description	Qty	Price	Discount	Total
☐						
☐						
☐						
☐						
☐						
☐						
☐						
☐						
☐						
☐						

TOTAL

Payment Details

Subtotal :

Delivery :

Discount:

TAX   :

Date

Total

Status

☐ Paid   ☐ Half Paid   ☐ Pending

Payment Method

☐ Cash   ☐ Credit Card   ☐ Bank   ☐ PayPal

☐ Other :

Special Notes

Delivery Details

Delivery Date :

Method   :   ☐ Pick-up   ☐ Delivery

Tracking No

Status

☐ Started   ☐ Finished   ☐ Delivered

Order Form - Small Orders

Name :

Address:

Phone: **Email :**

ORDER NO:

DATE:

ORDER NAME: ✓

Order Details

	#	Item/Description	Qty	Price	Discount	Total
☐						
☐						
☐						
☐						
☐						

Notes: **TOTAL**

Payment Details

Subtotal :

Delivery :

Discount: **TAX:**

Method :

Date

Total

Status
☐ Paid   ☐ Half Paid   ☐ Pending

Delivery Details

Delivery Date :

Method : ☐ Pick-up ☐ Delivery

Tracking No

Status
☐ Started   ☐ Finished   ☐ Delivered

Order Form - Small Orders

Name :

Address:

Phone: **Email :**

ORDER NO:

DATE:

ORDER NAME: ✓

Order Details

	#	Item/Description	Qty	Price	Discount	Total
☐						
☐						
☐						
☐						
☐						

Notes: **TOTAL**

Payment Details

Subtotal :

Delivery :

Discount: **TAX:**

Method :

Date

Total

Status
☐ Paid   ☐ Half Paid   ☐ Pending

Delivery Details

Delivery Date :

Method : ☐ Pick-up ☐ Delivery

Tracking No

Status
☐ Started   ☐ Finished   ☐ Delivered

Order Form

ORDER NO:

DATE:

ORDER NAME:

✓

Customer Details

Name :

Company:

Phone:

Email :

Address:

Order Details

	#	Item/Description	Qty	Price	Discount	Total
☐						
☐						
☐						
☐						
☐						
☐						
☐						
☐						
☐						
☐						

TOTAL

Payment Details

Subtotal :

Delivery :

Discount:

TAX :

Date

Total

Status

☐ Paid ☐ Half Paid ☐ Pending

Payment Method

☐ Cash ☐ Credit Card ☐ Bank ☐ PayPal

☐ Other :

Delivery Details

Delivery Date :

Method : ☐ Pick-up ☐ Delivery

Tracking No

Status

☐ Started ☐ Finished ☐ Delivered

Special Notes

Order Form

ORDER NO:

DATE:

ORDER NAME:

✓

Customer Details

Name :

Company:

Phone: Email :

Address:

Order Details

#	Item/Description	Qty	Price	Discount	Total
☐					
☐					
☐					
☐					
☐					
☐					
☐					
☐					
☐					
☐					

TOTAL

Payment Details

Subtotal :

Delivery :

Discount:

TAX   :

Date

Total

Status

☐ Paid ☐ Half Paid ☐ Pending

Payment Method

☐ Cash ☐ Credit Card ☐ Bank ☐ PayPal

☐ Other :

Delivery Details

Delivery Date :

Method   : ☐ Pick-up ☐ Delivery

Tracking No

Status

☐ Started ☐ Finished ☐ Delivered

Special Notes

Order Form

ORDER NO:

DATE:

ORDER NAME:

✓

Customer Details

Name :

Company:

Phone: Email :

Address:

Order Details

	#	Item/Description	Qty	Price	Discount	Total
☐						
☐						
☐						
☐						
☐						
☐						
☐						
☐						
☐						
☐						

TOTAL

Payment Details

Subtotal :

Delivery :

Discount :

TAX   :

Date

Total

Status
☐ Paid   ☐ Half Paid   ☐ Pending

Payment Method
☐ Cash   ☐ Credit Card   ☐ Bank   ☐ PayPal
☐ Other :

Special Notes

Delivery Details

Delivery Date :

Method   :   ☐ Pick-up   ☐ Delivery

Tracking No

Status
☐ Started   ☐ Finished   ☐ Delivered

Order Form - Small Orders

Name :

Address:

Phone: **Email :**

ORDER NO:

DATE:

ORDER NAME: ✓

Order Details

	#	Item/Description	Qty	Price	Discount	Total
☐						
☐						
☐						
☐						
☐						

Notes: **TOTAL**

Payment Details

Subtotal :

Delivery :

Discount: **TAX:**

Method :

Date

Total

Status
☐ Paid   ☐ Half Paid   ☐ Pending

Delivery Details

Delivery Date :

Method :   ☐ Pick-up   ☐ Delivery

Tracking No

Status
☐ Started   ☐ Finished   ☐ Delivered

Order Form - Small Orders

Name :

Address:

Phone: **Email :**

ORDER NO:

DATE:

ORDER NAME: ✓

Order Details

	#	Item/Description	Qty	Price	Discount	Total
☐						
☐						
☐						
☐						
☐						

Notes: **TOTAL**

Payment Details

Subtotal :

Delivery :

Discount: **TAX:**

Method :

Date

Total

Status
☐ Paid   ☐ Half Paid   ☐ Pending

Delivery Details

Delivery Date :

Method :   ☐ Pick-up   ☐ Delivery

Tracking No

Status
☐ Started   ☐ Finished   ☐ Delivered

Order Form

ORDER NO:

DATE:

ORDER NAME:

✓

Customer Details

Name :

Company:

Phone:

Email :

Address:

Order Details

	#	Item/Description	Qty	Price	Discount	Total
☐						
☐						
☐						
☐						
☐						
☐						
☐						
☐						
☐						
☐						
					TOTAL	

Payment Details

Subtotal :

Delivery :

Discount :

TAX :

Date

Total

Status

☐ Paid   ☐ Half Paid   ☐ Pending

Payment Method

☐ Cash   ☐ Credit Card   ☐ Bank   ☐ PayPal

☐ Other :

Special Notes

Delivery Details

Delivery Date :

Method : ☐ Pick-up   ☐ Delivery

Tracking No

Status

☐ Started   ☐ Finished   ☐ Delivered

Order Form

ORDER NO:

DATE:

ORDER NAME:

✓

Customer Details

Name :

Company:

Phone:

Email :

Address:

Order Details

#	Item/Description	Qty	Price	Discount	Total
☐					
☐					
☐					
☐					
☐					
☐					
☐					
☐					
☐					
☐					

TOTAL

Payment Details

Subtotal :

Delivery :

Discount :

TAX :

Date

Total

Status
☐ Paid ☐ Half Paid ☐ Pending

Payment Method
☐ Cash ☐ Credit Card ☐ Bank ☐ PayPal
☐ Other :

Special Notes

Delivery Details

Delivery Date :

Method : ☐ Pick-up ☐ Delivery

Tracking No

Status
☐ Started ☐ Finished ☐ Delivered

Order Form

ORDER NO:

DATE:

ORDER NAME:

✓

Customer Details

Name :

Address:

Company:

Phone:

Email :

Order Details

	#	Item/Description	Qty	Price	Discount	Total
☐						
☐						
☐						
☐						
☐						
☐						
☐						
☐						
☐						
☐						

TOTAL

Payment Details

Subtotal :

Delivery :

Discount :

TAX :

Date

Total

Status
☐ Paid ☐ Half Paid ☐ Pending

Payment Method
☐ Cash ☐ Credit Card ☐ Bank ☐ PayPal
☐ Other :

Special Notes

Delivery Details

Delivery Date :

Method : ☐ Pick-up ☐ Delivery

Tracking No

Status
☐ Started ☐ Finished ☐ Delivered

Order Form - Small Orders

Name : _____

Address: _____

Phone: _____ **Email :** _____

ORDER NO: [_____]

DATE: [_____]

ORDER NAME: [_____] ✓ [___]

Order Details

	#	Item/Description	Qty	Price	Discount	Total
☐						
☐						
☐						
☐						
☐						

Notes:　　　　　　　　　　　　　　　　**TOTAL** [_____]

Payment Details

Subtotal : _____

Delivery : _____

Discount: _____ **TAX:** _____

Method : _____

Date [_____]

Total [_____]

Status
☐ Paid　☐ Half Paid　☐ Pending

Delivery Details

Delivery Date : _____

Method : ☐ Pick-up　☐ Delivery

Tracking No [_____]

Status
☐ Started　☐ Finished　☐ Delivered

Order Form - Small Orders

Name : _____

Address: _____

Phone: _____ **Email :** _____

ORDER NO: [_____]

DATE: [_____]

ORDER NAME: [_____] ✓ [___]

Order Details

	#	Item/Description	Qty	Price	Discount	Total
☐						
☐						
☐						
☐						
☐						

Notes:　　　　　　　　　　　　　　　　**TOTAL** [_____]

Payment Details

Subtotal : _____

Delivery : _____

Discount: _____ **TAX:** _____

Method : _____

Date [_____]

Total [_____]

Status
☐ Paid　☐ Half Paid　☐ Pending

Delivery Details

Delivery Date : _____

Method : ☐ Pick-up　☐ Delivery

Tracking No [_____]

Status
☐ Started　☐ Finished　☐ Delivered

Order Form

ORDER NO:

DATE:

ORDER NAME:

✓

Customer Details

Name :

Company:

Phone:

Email :

Address:

Order Details

	#	Item/Description	Qty	Price	Discount	Total
☐						
☐						
☐						
☐						
☐						
☐						
☐						
☐						
☐						
☐						

TOTAL

Payment Details

Subtotal :

Delivery :

Discount:

TAX   :

Date

Total

Status
☐ Paid ☐ Half Paid ☐ Pending

Payment Method
☐ Cash ☐ Credit Card ☐ Bank ☐ PayPal
☐ Other :

Special Notes

Delivery Details

Delivery Date :

Method   : ☐ Pick-up ☐ Delivery

Tracking No

Status
☐ Started ☐ Finished ☐ Delivered

Order Form

ORDER NO:

DATE:

ORDER NAME:

✓

Customer Details

Name :

Company:

Phone:

Email :

Address:

Order Details

	#	Item/Description	Qty	Price	Discount	Total
☐						
☐						
☐						
☐						
☐						
☐						
☐						
☐						
☐						
☐						

TOTAL

Payment Details

Subtotal :

Delivery :

Discount :

TAX   :

Date

Total

Status

☐ Paid   ☐ Half Paid   ☐ Pending

Payment Method

☐ Cash   ☐ Credit Card   ☐ Bank   ☐ PayPal

☐ Other :

Delivery Details

Delivery Date :

Method   :   ☐ Pick-up   ☐ Delivery

Tracking No

Status

☐ Started   ☐ Finished   ☐ Delivered

Special Notes

Order Form

ORDER NO:

DATE:

ORDER NAME:

✓

Customer Details

Name :

Company:

Phone:

Email :

Address:

Order Details

	#	Item/Description	Qty	Price	Discount	Total
☐						
☐						
☐						
☐						
☐						
☐						
☐						
☐						
☐						
☐						

TOTAL

Payment Details

Subtotal :

Delivery :

Discount :

TAX :

Date

Total

Status

☐ Paid ☐ Half Paid ☐ Pending

Payment Method

☐ Cash ☐ Credit Card ☐ Bank ☐ PayPal

☐ Other :

Special Notes

Delivery Details

Delivery Date :

Method : ☐ Pick-up ☐ Delivery

Tracking No

Status

☐ Started ☐ Finished ☐ Delivered

Order Form - Small Orders

Name : _____

Address: _____

Phone: _____ **Email :** _____

ORDER NO: [   ] **DATE:** [   ]

ORDER NAME: [   ] ✓ [ ]

Order Details

#	Item/Description	Qty	Price	Discount	Total
[ ]					
[ ]					
[ ]					
[ ]					
[ ]					

Notes: | | **TOTAL** | [ ]

Payment Details

Subtotal : _____

Delivery : _____

Discount: _____ **TAX:** _____

Method : _____

Date [   ]

Total [   ]

Status
[ ] Paid   [ ] Half Paid   [ ] Pending

Delivery Details

Delivery Date : _____

Method : [ ] Pick-up [ ] Delivery

Tracking No [   ]

Status
[ ] Started   [ ] Finished   [ ] Delivered

Order Form - Small Orders

Name : _____

Address: _____

Phone: _____ **Email :** _____

ORDER NO: [   ] **DATE:** [   ]

ORDER NAME: [   ] ✓ [ ]

Order Details

#	Item/Description	Qty	Price	Discount	Total
[ ]					
[ ]					
[ ]					
[ ]					
[ ]					

Notes: | | **TOTAL** | [ ]

Payment Details

Subtotal : _____

Delivery : _____

Discount: _____ **TAX:** _____

Method : _____

Date [   ]

Total [   ]

Status
[ ] Paid   [ ] Half Paid   [ ] Pending

Delivery Details

Delivery Date : _____

Method : [ ] Pick-up [ ] Delivery

Tracking No [   ]

Status
[ ] Started   [ ] Finished   [ ] Delivered

Order Form

ORDER NO:

DATE:

ORDER NAME:

✓

Customer Details

Name :

Address:

Company:

Phone:

Email :

Order Details

#	Item/Description	Qty	Price	Discount	Total
☐					
☐					
☐					
☐					
☐					
☐					
☐					
☐					
☐					
☐					

TOTAL

Payment Details

Subtotal :

Delivery :

Discount:

TAX :

Date

Total

Status

☐ Paid ☐ Half Paid ☐ Pending

Payment Method

☐ Cash ☐ Credit Card ☐ Bank ☐ PayPal

☐ Other :

Special Notes

Delivery Details

Delivery Date :

Method : ☐ Pick-up ☐ Delivery

Tracking No

Status

☐ Started ☐ Finished ☐ Delivered

Order Form

ORDER NO:

DATE:

ORDER NAME:

✓

Customer Details

Name :

Address:

Company:

Phone:

Email :

Order Details

#	Item/Description	Qty	Price	Discount	Total
☐					
☐					
☐					
☐					
☐					
☐					
☐					
☐					
☐					
☐					
				TOTAL	

Payment Details

Subtotal :

Delivery :

Discount:

TAX   :

Date

Total

Status
☐ Paid   ☐ Half Paid   ☐ Pending

Payment Method
☐ Cash   ☐ Credit Card   ☐ Bank   ☐ PayPal
☐ Other :

Special Notes

Delivery Details

Delivery Date :

Method   :   ☐ Pick-up   ☐ Delivery

Tracking No

Status
☐ Started   ☐ Finished   ☐ Delivered

Order Form

ORDER NO:

DATE:

ORDER NAME:

✓

Customer Details

Name :

Company:

Phone: Email :

Address:

Order Details

#	Item/Description	Qty	Price	Discount	Total
☐					
☐					
☐					
☐					
☐					
☐					
☐					
☐					
☐					
☐					

TOTAL

Payment Details

Subtotal :

Delivery :

Discount:

TAX   :

Date

Total

Status
☐ Paid   ☐ Half Paid   ☐ Pending

Payment Method
☐ Cash   ☐ Credit Card   ☐ Bank   ☐ PayPal
☐ Other :

Special Notes

Delivery Details

Delivery Date :

Method   :   ☐ Pick-up   ☐ Delivery

Tracking No

Status
☐ Started   ☐ Finished   ☐ Delivered

Order Form - Small Orders

ORDER NO:

DATE:

Name :

Address:

Phone:　　　　Email :

ORDER NAME:

✓

Order Details

#	Item/Description	Qty	Price	Discount	Total
☐					
☐					
☐					
☐					
☐					

Notes: **TOTAL**

Payment Details

Subtotal :

Delivery :

Discount:　　TAX:

Method :

Date

Total

Status
☐ Paid　☐ Half Paid　☐ Pending

Delivery Details

Delivery Date :

Method　　　: ☐ Pick-up　☐ Delivery

Tracking No

Status
☐ Started　☐ Finished　☐ Delivered

Order Form - Small Orders

ORDER NO:

DATE:

Name :

Address:

Phone:　　　　Email :

ORDER NAME:

✓

Order Details

#	Item/Description	Qty	Price	Discount	Total
☐					
☐					
☐					
☐					
☐					

Notes: **TOTAL**

Payment Details

Subtotal :

Delivery :

Discount:　　TAX:

Method :

Date

Total

Status
☐ Paid　☐ Half Paid　☐ Pending

Delivery Details

Delivery Date :

Method　　　: ☐ Pick-up　☐ Delivery

Tracking No

Status
☐ Started　☐ Finished　☐ Delivered

Order Form

ORDER NO:

DATE:

ORDER NAME:

✓

Customer Details

Name :

Address:

Company:

Phone:

Email :

Order Details

	#	Item/Description	Qty	Price	Discount	Total
☐						
☐						
☐						
☐						
☐						
☐						
☐						
☐						
☐						
☐						

TOTAL

Payment Details

Subtotal :

Delivery :

Discount :

TAX :

Date

Total

Status

☐ Paid ☐ Half Paid ☐ Pending

Payment Method

☐ Cash ☐ Credit Card ☐ Bank ☐ PayPal

☐ Other :

Special Notes

Delivery Details

Delivery Date :

Method : ☐ Pick-up ☐ Delivery

Tracking No

Status

☐ Started ☐ Finished ☐ Delivered

Order Form

ORDER NO:

DATE:

ORDER NAME:

✓

Customer Details

Name :

Address:

Company:

Phone:

Email :

Order Details

#	Item/Description	Qty	Price	Discount	Total
☐					
☐					
☐					
☐					
☐					
☐					
☐					
☐					
☐					
☐					

TOTAL

Payment Details

Subtotal :

Delivery :

Discount :

TAX :

Date

Total

Status

☐ Paid ☐ Half Paid ☐ Pending

Payment Method

☐ Cash ☐ Credit Card ☐ Bank ☐ PayPal

☐ Other :

Delivery Details

Delivery Date :

Method : ☐ Pick-up ☐ Delivery

Tracking No

Status

☐ Started ☐ Finished ☐ Delivered

Special Notes

Order Form

ORDER NO:

DATE:

ORDER NAME:

✓

Customer Details

Name :

Address:

Company:

Phone:

Email :

Order Details

	#	Item/Description	Qty	Price	Discount	Total
☐						
☐						
☐						
☐						
☐						
☐						
☐						
☐						
☐						
☐						

TOTAL

Payment Details

Subtotal :

Delivery :

Discount:

TAX :

Date

Total

Status
☐ Paid ☐ Half Paid ☐ Pending

Payment Method
☐ Cash ☐ Credit Card ☐ Bank ☐ PayPal
☐ Other :

Special Notes

Delivery Details

Delivery Date :

Method : ☐ Pick-up ☐ Delivery

Tracking No

Status
☐ Started ☐ Finished ☐ Delivered

Order Form - Small Orders

Name :

Address:

Phone: **Email :**

ORDER NO:

DATE:

ORDER NAME: ✓

Order Details

#	Item/Description	Qty	Price	Discount	Total
☐					
☐					
☐					
☐					
☐					

Notes: **TOTAL**

Payment Details

Subtotal :

Delivery :

Discount: **TAX:**

Method :

Date

Total

Status
☐ Paid   ☐ Half Paid   ☐ Pending

Delivery Details

Delivery Date :

Method   : ☐ Pick-up   ☐ Delivery

Tracking No

Status
☐ Started   ☐ Finished   ☐ Delivered

Order Form - Small Orders

Name :

Address:

Phone: **Email :**

ORDER NO:

DATE:

ORDER NAME: ✓

Order Details

#	Item/Description	Qty	Price	Discount	Total
☐					
☐					
☐					
☐					
☐					

Notes: **TOTAL**

Payment Details

Subtotal :

Delivery :

Discount: **TAX:**

Method :

Date

Total

Status
☐ Paid   ☐ Half Paid   ☐ Pending

Delivery Details

Delivery Date :

Method   : ☐ Pick-up   ☐ Delivery

Tracking No

Status
☐ Started   ☐ Finished   ☐ Delivered

Order Form

ORDER NO:

DATE:

ORDER NAME:

✓ ☐

Customer Details

Name : _____

Company: _____

Phone: _____ Email : _____

Address: _____

_____

Order Details

☐	#	Item/Description	Qty	Price	Discount	Total
☐						
☐						
☐						
☐						
☐						
☐						
☐						
☐						
☐						
☐						

TOTAL

Payment Details

Subtotal : _____

Delivery : _____

Discount : _____

TAX : _____

Date

Total

Status
☐ Paid ☐ Half Paid ☐ Pending

Payment Method
☐ Cash ☐ Credit Card ☐ Bank ☐ PayPal

☐ Other :

Delivery Details

Delivery Date : _____

Method : ☐ Pick-up ☐ Delivery

Tracking No

Status
☐ Started ☐ Finished ☐ Delivered

Special Notes

Order Form

ORDER NO:

DATE:

ORDER NAME:

✓

Customer Details

Name :

Address:

Company:

Phone:

Email :

Order Details

	#	Item/Description	Qty	Price	Discount	Total
☐						
☐						
☐						
☐						
☐						
☐						
☐						
☐						
☐						
☐						

TOTAL

Payment Details

Subtotal :

Delivery :

Discount :

TAX :

Date

Total

Status

☐ Paid   ☐ Half Paid   ☐ Pending

Payment Method

☐ Cash   ☐ Credit Card   ☐ Bank   ☐ PayPal

☐ Other :

Special Notes

Delivery Details

Delivery Date :

Method   :   ☐ Pick-up   ☐ Delivery

Tracking No

Status

☐ Started   ☐ Finished   ☐ Delivered

Order Form

ORDER NO:

DATE:

ORDER NAME:

✓

Customer Details

Name :

Address:

Company:

Phone:

Email :

Order Details

☐	#	Item/Description	Qty	Price	Discount	Total
☐						
☐						
☐						
☐						
☐						
☐						
☐						
☐						
☐						
☐						

TOTAL

Payment Details

Subtotal :

Delivery :

Discount:

TAX   :

Date

Total

Status
☐ Paid ☐ Half Paid ☐ Pending

Payment Method
☐ Cash ☐ Credit Card ☐ Bank ☐ PayPal
☐ Other :

Special Notes

Delivery Details

Delivery Date :

Method   : ☐ Pick-up ☐ Delivery

Tracking No

Status
☐ Started ☐ Finished ☐ Delivered

Order Form - Small Orders

Name :

Address:

Phone: **Email :**

ORDER NO:

DATE:

ORDER NAME: ✓

Order Details

#	Item/Description	Qty	Price	Discount	Total
☐					
☐					
☐					
☐					
☐					

Notes: **TOTAL**

Payment Details

Subtotal :

Delivery :

Discount: **TAX:**

Method :

Date

Total

Status
☐ Paid ☐ Half Paid ☐ Pending

Delivery Details

Delivery Date :

Method : ☐ Pick-up ☐ Delivery

Tracking No

Status
☐ Started ☐ Finished ☐ Delivered

Order Form - Small Orders

Name :

Address:

Phone: **Email :**

ORDER NO:

DATE:

ORDER NAME: ✓

Order Details

#	Item/Description	Qty	Price	Discount	Total
☐					
☐					
☐					
☐					
☐					

Notes: **TOTAL**

Payment Details

Subtotal :

Delivery :

Discount: **TAX:**

Method :

Date

Total

Status
☐ Paid ☐ Half Paid ☐ Pending

Delivery Details

Delivery Date :

Method : ☐ Pick-up ☐ Delivery

Tracking No

Status
☐ Started ☐ Finished ☐ Delivered

Order Form

ORDER NO:

DATE:

ORDER NAME:

✓

Customer Details

Name :

Address:

Company:

Phone:

Email :

Order Details

	#	Item/Description	Qty	Price	Discount	Total
☐						
☐						
☐						
☐						
☐						
☐						
☐						
☐						
☐						
☐						

TOTAL

Payment Details

Subtotal :

Delivery :

Discount :

TAX :

Date

Total

Status

☐ Paid   ☐ Half Paid   ☐ Pending

Payment Method

☐ Cash   ☐ Credit Card   ☐ Bank   ☐ PayPal

☐ Other :

Delivery Details

Delivery Date :

Method : ☐ Pick-up   ☐ Delivery

Tracking No

Status

☐ Started   ☐ Finished   ☐ Delivered

Special Notes

Order Form

ORDER NO:

DATE:

ORDER NAME:

✓

Customer Details

Name :

Address:

Company:

Phone:

Email :

Order Details

#	Item/Description	Qty	Price	Discount	Total
☐					
☐					
☐					
☐					
☐					
☐					
☐					
☐					
☐					
☐					

TOTAL

Payment Details

Subtotal :

Delivery :

Discount :

TAX :

Date

Total

Status

☐ Paid   ☐ Half Paid   ☐ Pending

Payment Method

☐ Cash   ☐ Credit Card   ☐ Bank   ☐ PayPal

☐ Other :

Delivery Details

Delivery Date :

Method : ☐ Pick-up   ☐ Delivery

Tracking No

Status

☐ Started   ☐ Finished   ☐ Delivered

Special Notes

Order Form

ORDER NO:

DATE:

ORDER NAME:

✓

Customer Details

Name :

Address:

Company:

Phone:

Email :

Order Details

	#	Item/Description	Qty	Price	Discount	Total
☐						
☐						
☐						
☐						
☐						
☐						
☐						
☐						
☐						
☐						

TOTAL

Payment Details

Subtotal :

Delivery :

Discount :

TAX :

Date

Total

Status

☐ Paid ☐ Half Paid ☐ Pending

Payment Method

☐ Cash ☐ Credit Card ☐ Bank ☐ PayPal

☐ Other :

Special Notes

Delivery Details

Delivery Date :

Method : ☐ Pick-up ☐ Delivery

Tracking No

Status

☐ Started ☐ Finished ☐ Delivered

Order Form - Small Orders

Name :

Address:

Phone: **Email :**

ORDER NO:

DATE:

ORDER NAME: ✓

Order Details

#	Item/Description	Qty	Price	Discount	Total
☐					
☐					
☐					
☐					
☐					

Notes: **TOTAL**

Payment Details

Subtotal :

Delivery :

Discount: **TAX:**

Method :

Date

Total

Status
☐ Paid   ☐ Half Paid   ☐ Pending

Delivery Details

Delivery Date :

Method :   ☐ Pick-up   ☐ Delivery

Tracking No

Status
☐ Started   ☐ Finished   ☐ Delivered

Order Form - Small Orders

Name :

Address:

Phone: **Email :**

ORDER NO:

DATE:

ORDER NAME: ✓

Order Details

#	Item/Description	Qty	Price	Discount	Total
☐					
☐					
☐					
☐					
☐					

Notes: **TOTAL**

Payment Details

Subtotal :

Delivery :

Discount: **TAX:**

Method :

Date

Total

Status
☐ Paid   ☐ Half Paid   ☐ Pending

Delivery Details

Delivery Date :

Method :   ☐ Pick-up   ☐ Delivery

Tracking No

Status
☐ Started   ☐ Finished   ☐ Delivered

Order Form

ORDER NO:

DATE:

ORDER NAME:

✓

Customer Details

Name :

Company:

Phone:

Email :

Address:

Order Details

	#	Item/Description	Qty	Price	Discount	Total
☐						
☐						
☐						
☐						
☐						
☐						
☐						
☐						
☐						
☐						

TOTAL

Payment Details

Subtotal :

Delivery :

Discount :

TAX   :

Date

Total

Status
☐ Paid   ☐ Half Paid   ☐ Pending

Payment Method
☐ Cash   ☐ Credit Card   ☐ Bank   ☐ PayPal
☐ Other :

Delivery Details

Delivery Date :

Method   :   ☐ Pick-up   ☐ Delivery

Tracking No

Status
☐ Started   ☐ Finished   ☐ Delivered

Special Notes

Order Form

ORDER NO:

DATE:

ORDER NAME:

✓

Customer Details

Name :

Company:

Phone: Email :

Address:

Order Details

#	Item/Description	Qty	Price	Discount	Total
☐					
☐					
☐					
☐					
☐					
☐					
☐					
☐					
☐					
☐					

TOTAL

Payment Details

Subtotal :

Delivery :

Discount :

TAX   :

Date

Total

Status

☐ Paid   ☐ Half Paid   ☐ Pending

Payment Method

☐ Cash   ☐ Credit Card   ☐ Bank   ☐ PayPal

☐ Other :

Delivery Details

Delivery Date :

Method   :   ☐ Pick-up   ☐ Delivery

Tracking No

Status

☐ Started   ☐ Finished   ☐ Delivered

Special Notes

Order Form

ORDER NO:

DATE:

ORDER NAME:

✓

Customer Details

Name :

Address:

Company:

Phone:

Email :

Order Details

#	Item/Description	Qty	Price	Discount	Total
☐					
☐					
☐					
☐					
☐					
☐					
☐					
☐					
☐					
☐					

TOTAL

Payment Details

Subtotal :

Delivery :

Discount:

TAX :

Date

Total

Status

☐ Paid ☐ Half Paid ☐ Pending

Payment Method

☐ Cash ☐ Credit Card ☐ Bank ☐ PayPal

☐ Other :

Delivery Details

Delivery Date :

Method : ☐ Pick-up ☐ Delivery

Tracking No

Status

☐ Started ☐ Finished ☐ Delivered

Special Notes

Order Form - Small Orders

Name :

Address:

Phone: **Email :**

ORDER NO:

DATE:

ORDER NAME: ✓

Order Details

#	Item/Description	Qty	Price	Discount	Total
☐					
☐					
☐					
☐					
☐					

Notes: **TOTAL**

Payment Details

Subtotal :

Delivery :

Discount: **TAX:**

Method :

Date

Total

Status
☐ Paid   ☐ Half Paid   ☐ Pending

Delivery Details

Delivery Date :

Method :   ☐ Pick-up   ☐ Delivery

Tracking No

Status
☐ Started   ☐ Finished   ☐ Delivered

Order Form - Small Orders

Name :

Address:

Phone: **Email :**

ORDER NO:

DATE:

ORDER NAME: ✓

Order Details

#	Item/Description	Qty	Price	Discount	Total
☐					
☐					
☐					
☐					
☐					

Notes: **TOTAL**

Payment Details

Subtotal :

Delivery :

Discount: **TAX:**

Method :

Date

Total

Status
☐ Paid   ☐ Half Paid   ☐ Pending

Delivery Details

Delivery Date :

Method :   ☐ Pick-up   ☐ Delivery

Tracking No

Status
☐ Started   ☐ Finished   ☐ Delivered

Made in the USA
Monee, IL
04 November 2024

69246016R00111